THE DRAGON'S
TEETH

JOHN ROBERT YOUNG

THE DRAGON'S
INSIDE CHINA'S ARMED FORCES
TEETH

Hutchinson

London Melbourne Auckland Johannesburg

For my dear mother

Designed and produced by John Calmann and King Ltd
71 Great Russell Street, London WC1B 3BN

Designers Karen Osborne and Roy Trevelion

This edition first published in 1987 by Hutchinson, an imprint of
Century Hutchinson Ltd, Brookmount House, 62–65 Chandos Place, London
WC2N 4NW

Century Hutchinson Australia Pty Ltd
PO Box 496, 16–22 Church Street, Hawthorn, Victoria 3122, Australia

Century Hutchinson New Zealand Limited
PO Box 40–086, Glenfield, Auckland 10, New Zealand

Century Hutchinson South Africa (Pty) Ltd
PO Box 337, Berglvei, 2012 South Africa

British Library Cataloguing in Publication Data

Young, John Robert
   The dragon's teeth: inside China's armed forces.
   1. China — Zhong guo ren min jie fang jun
   I. Title
   355'.00951   DA839.3

   ISBN 0-09-170680-7

Printed and bound in the Netherlands by
Royal Smeets Offset bv Weert

Contents

Photographic Notes

Ideally I would like to travel the world with two Leica rangefinder cameras and four lenses: 21 mm, 35 mm, 50 mm and 90 mm tucked away in one of my many stout, if dilapidated, canvas bags.

Over the years I have used numerous cameras: cumbersome Speed Graphics, umpteen different roll-film cameras, as well as the current crop of Japanese 35 mm cameras. The tough, rugged Leica – rangefinder and SLR – is the finest equipment for my work as a reportage and documentary photographer. Images from the Leitz lenses are subtle and perfectly colour-balanced, with none of the harshness of some modern-day Japanese optics.

Usually I like to travel as lightly as possible. For my China project, however, equipment had to be far more comprehensive. Metal cases were purchased and specially tailored to accept all my camera bodies and lenses, as all my equipment would have to be transported in aircraft cargo holds.

Finally, after days of considering every possible combination, my equipment consisted of:

Three Leica R4 S bodies with motors; two fitted with handles, a most useful accessory I find when working. My lenses were: 16 mm; 19 mm; 24 mm; 35 mm; 50 mm; 60 mm macro; 90 mm; 180 mm; and 400 mm.

Two Leica rangefinder cameras, models M4 and M6, with the following lenses: 21 mm; 28 mm; 35 mm; and the superb 50 mm 1.4 Summilux.

Accessories included: filters; various brushes and chamois (for cleaning); cable release; Swiss army knife; selection of watchmakers' screwdrivers; a small flash; tripod; X2 doubler; and various filters.

Three meters: Weston Master IV; Minolta III; and Minolta Spotmeter.

Four hundred rolls of colour film were packed into a medium-sized holdall and travelled with me on board the aircraft. A small canvas bag was included in my personal luggage to carry the day's working equipment.

My daily working equipment could consist of: two camera bodies; four lenses; a meter; and twenty to thirty rolls of film, depending on the locations for the day.

Acknowledgements

No one person produces a book. Without the co-operation, kindness and generosity of the following people, each contributing their own expertise, this book would not have been possible.

Mr Feng Zhenyao and Mr Chen Wen Qing, both Military Attachés at the London Embassy of the People's Republic of China.

In China I was in the care of Mr Gu Jingshu, of the Foreign Affairs Bureau at the Ministry of Defence in Peking. He was not only my interpreter, but also my guide and travelling companion. Mr Gu secured plane and train reservations, made endless phone calls to regimental commanders, steered me through security and X-ray machines, made sure I had somewhere to lay my head, and, wherever possible, western food to eat. My other travelling companion was Mr Chen Detung, a senior member of the staff of the PLA Pictorial. Ever smiling and cheerful, he spent many hours retrieving archival negatives and supervised their printing for reproduction. During our travels he carried camera bags, equipment and film, so lightening my burden when working under pressure.

The International Institute of Strategic Studies, London and their publications have been used as a prime source for all military statistical information in this book. I would also like to thank the staff for their helpful advice.

General Sir Anthony Farrar-Hockley, GBE, KCB, DSO and Bar, MC gave of his time without reservation to discuss the PLA and his service with the Gloucestershire Regiment in Korea, when he was Adjutant with the First Battalion. As a prisoner of the Chinese (CPV) he made six escape attempts. Sinologist, Bob Sloss, Dean of Darwin College, Cambridge, was immensely helpful in confirming Chinese political trends together with his assessment of the PLA.

Further background material on Korea was kindly recalled for me by former members of the Gloucestershire Regiment: Major Paul Baldwin Mitchell; former Drum Major, now Mr Philip Edward Buss; and former sniper, Albert Edward Marsh, MM. The Glosters held out against overwhelming odds until their ammunition was exhausted, on now forgotten ridges overlooking the Imjin River.

Carol Adelson and Belinda Flood worked all hours dutifully transcribing my near illegible copy into beautiful manuscript form.

Jennifer, my wife, painstakingly edited my first drafts, and daily provided comfort and inspiration throughout the months of editorial ramifications.

Esther Sampson (Cheo Ying), a former member of the Fourth Army, supplied me with unique eye-witness material. She must surely be the only woman in Britain today who has served in the ranks of the PLA.

Richard Cohen, my publisher, who from the outset never wavered in his confidence that I would ultimately return from what many regarded as a perilous undertaking.

I also wish to express my appreciation to Kate Mosse, my editor, who so diligently enhanced and streamlined my text.

Finally, there were people I met along the way who, regretfully, I cannot name or portray. For their advice, counsel and confidence, I am ever grateful.

Preface

Some dozen or more years ago during an assignment to Macau, I had been intrigued by a small fleet of junks and coastal patrol boats swaying against the incoming tide at their moorings in the harbour. The brilliant red flag with its yellow star told me that they had come from what we used to call Red China. A few years later in the New Territories – that extension of Hong Kong which reaches into the Chinese mainland – I peered across the rice paddies of Guangdong Province towards Canton just as the last rays of sunlight were disappearing behind the distant hills, and wondered how long it would be before I could explore China with the freedom I needed. For me China was a secret and forbidding land of a bygone age with mandarins, jade, and majestic sloe-eyed women.

More than a billion people, a quarter of the world's population, live in China, most of whom are sandwiched between the Bo Hai Gulf in the North, and the upper and lower reaches of the Yangtze River in the South. Regardless of the government's one child per family policy, a baby is born every two seconds. China's land mass covers over three million square miles, with weather ranging from the arctic to the monsoon. Footweary travellers avoid Peking's summer months; apart from a few weeks in autumn, its weather makes it one of the world's most uncomfortable capitals. The country's strength and power lies in its people. Since the birth of the Communist State in October 1949, opium-taking is unheard of, literacy has advanced, begging in the city streets is almost unknown, and there is a plentiful supply of food. Although it would be foolhardy to imply that all feudal practices have been eradicated, most of these age-old hideous customs have ceased as common practice.

China's two-thousand-year-old Great Wall is said to be one of the few geographical features that astronauts recognize during space flights. The wall meanders for more than two thousand miles, from the North-East coast north of Peking, to Jiayuguan in Gansu Province. Beyond is the desolate and scorched desert landscape of Mongolia.

China has the world's largest fighting force: an army, an air force and a navy, known collectively as the People's Liberation Army. At the Ministry of Defence in Peking, current policy regarding the PLA is modernization and restructuring, and it would appear that the long-awaited return to military ranking has met with opposition, from either the politicians, or the old army hands who have still to be caught up in the military's redundancy programme. As it was during its Red Army days, the PLA is still a political and ideological breeding ground, irrespective of the popular doctrine channelled from Peking that 'the Party controls the gun'.

As a military autocracy, China is extremely sensitive about the PLA or, for that matter, anything connected with her military forces. Whilst we in Britain have grown accustomed to military 'open days' when the public can view our armed forces at close quarters, no such opportunity exists in China.

It was in January 1985 that I first went to see the Chinese Military Attaché in London. Would his government allow me into the PLA with my cameras and tape recorder to gather material for a book, I asked him. To my surprise he appeared neither alarmed nor taken aback by my suggestions and, contrary to expectations, my proposal was not dismissed out of hand. Over the following months, my spirits would ebb and flow between a succession of meetings, phone calls and continual correspondence with the Chinese. I grew accustomed to none of my letters being answered, and it was not until early summer 1986 that I finally left for Peking, having been given a visa only a few days previously. It had taken seventeen months of patient waiting to be allowed inside the People's Liberation Army.

China watchers in the West have written in detail concerning the liberal 'open door' to China. However, it would be well to regard the open door with more than just a mild degree of caution. While it may be understandable for tourists to stray into previously unseen areas, in the case of a journalist a far more serious view is taken. Within a few days of my return to Britain, the *New York Times* correspondent in Peking, John F. Burns, was arrested in a restricted area, under what the Chinese Public Security Bureau regarded as 'unacceptable circumstances'. He was detained, questioned at some length, and finally deported for alleged spying activities. It was an incident which I am sure blew a wind of caution to all journalists resident in Peking. China is apprehensive about reporters, especially those of us who tell our stories with the camera.

On almost all of my journeys I was accompanied by two officials of the People's Republic of China. No matter where you are working in the world, securing your images and interviews, searching for locations, maintaining equipment, as well as making travel arrangements, is always tiring enough. But as a photojournalist in China, you have the added difficulties of endless discussions and negotiations with officialdom. Unless you can speak Chinese, your interpreter is your only linguistic avenue to the outside world: without the interpreter you are without communication, cut off from the China you wish to reach.

In my own case the many units of the PLA I visited received me with great enthusiasm. Their hospitality and personal care were remarkable. As it was the first time that the PLA had allowed a Western photojournalist to probe beneath the surface in such detail, they were, on the one hand, noticeably nervous of revealing their military lifestyle in too liberal a manner and, on the other, anxious to please and show themselves in the very best light. But it was within a very controlled framework that I was able to move with my cameras. It was a delicate balance, a daily exercise in diplomacy and courtesy towards my hosts. To offend could well have meant the rescinding of my facilities or, at the very least, a curtailment of them.

During the time I was with the men and women of the PLA, it was impossible not to admire their dedication and sense of purpose. The Chinese people have an infectious friendship and generosity which they shared with me on many occasions during the making of this book.

This is not a political work, although the PLA is soaked in political intrigue. Neither am I a Sinologist nor a military expert: there are those who are far better qualified than I to explain China's political role in the world today. It was as a documentarian that I entered the PLA. My

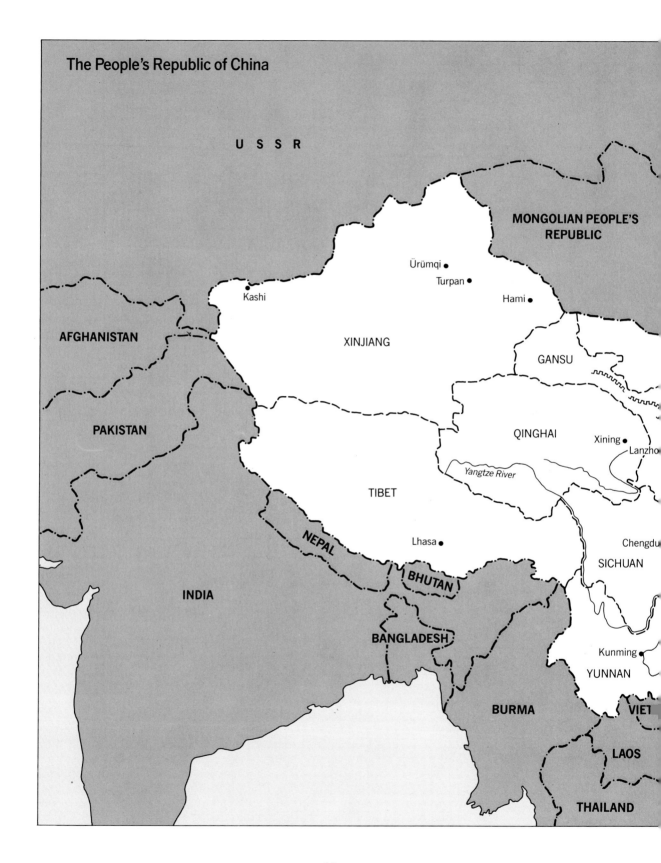

The People's Republic of China

U S S R

MONGOLIAN PEOPLE'S REPUBLIC

Ürümqi ●
Turpan ●
Kashi ●
Hami ●

AFGHANISTAN

XINJIANG

GANSU

PAKISTAN

QINGHAI

Xining ●
Lanzho●

Yangtze River

TIBET

Lhasa ●

Chengdu

SICHUAN

NEPAL

BHUTAN

INDIA

BANGLADESH

Kunming ●

YUNNAN

BURMA

VIET

LAOS

THAILAND

10

HEILONGJIANG

Daqing
Harbin

Changchun

INNER MONGOLIA   JILIN

Shenzhen
LIAONING

Baotou
Hohhot   GREAT WALL   PEKING
Yellow River   Taiyuan   Luda
HEBEI   BO HAI GULF

chuan   Shijiazhuang

GXIA   Tianjin   Jinan   Qingdao
SHANXI   SHANDONG

Luoyang   Changzhi   Kaifeng   JIANGSU
Xi'an   Zhengzhou

SHAANXI   HENAN   ANHUI
Nanjing
Hefei   Suzhou   Shanghai
HUBEI   Ningbo
Wuhan   Hangzhou

Chongqing   ZHEJIANG
Jingdezhen
HUNAN
GUIZHOU   Changsha   Nanchang
Guiyang   JIANGXI   Fuzhou
Guilin   FUJIAN
GUANGXI   Xiamen
West River   GUANGDONG
Nanning   Canton   Chaozhou   TAIWAN STRAIT   TAIPEI   TAIWAN
Shenyang

MACAO   HONG KONG

LF OF NKIN   Hainan Island
SOUTH CHINA SEA   PHILIPPINES

PEOPLE'S DEMOCRATIC REPUBLIC OF KOREA
REPUBLIC OF KOREA
JAPAN

YELLOW SEA

EAST CHINA SEA

Taipei

0   500 km
0   500 miles

cameras were to reveal as much as was permissible. China is still a secret and repressive land. Under its enigmatic surface, unseen by the Western world, the power struggles continue like some simmering witches' brew. This is a time of considerable development and change within China's military system and there is little doubt in my mind that the PLA will play a major role in her political and economic future.

Finally, the judgements and conclusions in this book are entirely my own. I have adopted no one particular system for the romanizing of Chinese characters, choosing rather to use the form which would be most easily recognizable to my readers, except when quoting Chinese people I met where I have retained those names used by the speaker.

PART 1
HISTORICAL
BACKGROUND

Chronology

600,000 BC–400,000 BC
Early civilization – Lantian Man, Peking Man – hominids occupy China's Yellow River Valley; use stone tools and fire.

4500 BC–2500 BC
Painted earthenware produced in China's North-West Province of Gansu.

XIA DYNASTY   c 2200 BC–1766 BC
Chinese records indicate possible existence of first dynasty – the Xia.

SHANG DYNASTY   c 1766 BC–1122 BC
First verifiable dynasty. Events and customs pictured on tortoise shells and bones. First writing. Evidence of the wheel and bronze emerge.

ZHOU DYNASTY   c 1122 BC–221 BC
Feudal states gain power after 771 BC. Great philosophers appear – Confucius (551 BC–479 BC) and Mencius (372 BC–289 BC). Development also in classical literature and arts. First canals begun.

QIN DYNASTY   c 221 BC–206 BC
China unified during this, one of the shortest dynasties. First Emperor combines regional walls to form the Great Wall. Constructs palaces, canals and roads. Standardized weights, measures and writing.

HAN DYNASTY   c 206 BC–AD 220
In this 400-year-long dynasty scientific and technological progress brings about the invention of paper, the compass and seismograph. A form of Civil Service is established. Buddhism finds its way into China from Central Asia, along the silk routes.

THREE KINGDOMS   AD 220–589
A long period of instability. Han generals become warlords and divide the empire.

SUI DYNASTY   AD 589–618
China reunited. Grand canal built.

TANG DYNASTY   AD 618–907
Changan, the ancient capital, rebuilt in the Sui Dynasty, becomes a cosmopolitan centre. Arts and scholarship flourish. Height of the silk trade.

SONG DYNASTY   AD 960–1279
Northern barbarians drive Song Government into Southern China. A commercial age.

YUAN DYNASTY   AD 1279–1368
The Mongol Conquest. Genghis Khan invades China. By 1263 Peking is the centre of the Mongol Empire.

MING DYNASTY   AD 1368–1644
Mongols defeated. Stable and prosperous era under strong emperors. Forbidden City and imperial tombs built. Dynasty also known for its superb porcelain. Maritime exploration into South-East Asia commences. Jesuits arrive.

QING DYNASTY   AD 1644–1911
Manchu overthrow Mongols – the Qing, China's last imperial dynasty, is established. Surrounding countries, such as Mongolia, Tibet, Korea and Annam are influenced by Chinese thinking. Europeans introduce opium. International forces subdue the 'Boxer Rebellion'. Dowager Empress Ci Xi dies and boy Emperor Puyi abdicates.

1911
10 October the outbreak of the Chinese Revolution. Dr Sun Yat-sen serves briefly as the first President of the Kuomintang (KMT) or Nationalist Party. He is forced to step down owing to the superior political and military strength of Yuan Shikai, a former Chief of the Imperial Armies.

1916
Yuan's plans for a new imperial dynasty are curtailed by his sudden death.

1921
Sees the founding of the Chinese Communist Party in Shanghai, aided by Russians who had

Party in Shanghai, aided by Russians who had participated in the Bolshevik Revolution.

1925–31

Dr Sun Yat-sen dies and Chiang Kai-shek leads the KMT. Following a brief period of co-operation Chiang severs his working relationship with the Communists.

On August 1 1927, revolutionaries, led by Chou Enlai and Chu Teh, stage the unsuccessful Nanchang Uprising. This is regarded in China's history as the date when the Red Army was inaugurated.

In September 1927, Mao Tse-tung organizes the short-lived 'Autumn Harvest Uprising' using the first units of the peasant worker army. Other areas of the country come under control of the Communists.

1934–6

Due to overwhelming pressure from KMT forces, the Communists' units are forced to retreat to China's Shaanxi Province. This is known as the Long March period.

1937–45

Second Sino-Japanese War. America declares war on Japan following the bombing of Pearl Harbour, and gives aid to Nationalist forces. Japan surrenders.

1946–9

Civil War, now known as the War of Liberation, recommences between the Communists and the KMT. Communist forces overwhelm the KMT and Chiang Kai-shek flees to Taiwan, where he sets up a government in exile.

1949–58

On October 1 1949, Mao Tse-tung proclaims People's Republic of China. Private land is redistributed to the peasants. PLA 'volunteers' fight in the Korean War.

1958

'The Great Leap Forward' – agrarian reform, farming communes organized. This ill-fated plan culminated in the withdrawal of all Soviet economic and military aid from China.

1966

The beginning of the Great Proletarian Revolution, the effects of which last for a decade. Several PLA commanders are vilified during this period.

In 1971 the People's Republic of China is admitted to the United Nations and obtains a place on the Security Council.

1976

Premier Chou Enlai and Chairman Mao Tse-tung die. The Gang of Four is arrested.

1981

The new Chinese leaders emerge: Hua Guofeng, Hu Yaobang, Zhao Ziyang and Deng Xiaoping.

Radical reorganization of the People's Liberation Army – many senior generals and officers are 'retired'. The PLA embarks upon programme of re-education with special attention to Western high technology. Defence spending is moderated by the current programme of the four modernizations.

PLA representatives visit major Western countries to update their knowledge of Western technology.

1986–7

Student demonstrations in December 1986 and January 1987 demanding greater 'liberalization' from the government in several Chinese cities. Those in Peking and Shanghai reported to be the largest since the Cultural Revolution of twenty years ago. The Party demands the purging of leading intellectuals, referring to them as 'troublesome bourgeois liberals'.

Hu Yaobang, Secretary General of the Chinese Communist Party, forced to resign: the highest ranking Party member to be purged in the last ten years. He is replaced by Premier Zhao Ziyang.

China's Military and Political Leaders

Chiang Kai-shek

Leader of the Kuomintang and President of China, he was Mao Tse-tung's chief adversary. Born in 1887 in Zhejiang Province, the son of a peasant, he obtained his military training with the Japanese, and graduated from a Japanese military school in 1909. It was in Japan that he came into contact with Sun Yat-sen who brought him into the Nationalist Party. He became the first President of the Whampoa Military Academy in Canton, at that time the foremost officer training establishment in China. In 1927 he married the sister of Madam Sun Yat-sen. Throughout his life he was obsessed with exterminating the Communists. In September 1945 Chiang was elected President of the Chinese Republic. Lethargy, corruption and a series of military disasters against the Communists led to his downfall. Defeated, Generalissimo Chiang Kai-shek fled to Taiwan with the remnants of his Kuomintang forces. He died there in 1975.

Chou Enlai

On the formation of the Chinese People's Republic, Chou Enlai was concurrently Premier and Foreign Minister. He was born in 1898 and died in 1976.

Chou Enlai must be regarded as China's foremost pragmatist and diplomat since the beginning of the communist movement. He was, among all of China's leaders, the man with whom the West could both communicate and trust; he understood Western attitudes better than any of his contemporaries.

Like many of China's leaders who emerged through the nationalist and communist movements, he studied in Paris and made several visits to Moscow. Throughout his life-time Chou Enlai was held in high regard by all factions within the Chinese Communist Party. From his earliest days as a Communist he was seen as a man endowed with great leadership potential. A notable example of Chou's diplomacy was at the Zunyi conference in

January 1935; he confessed to making strategic errors during the fifth encirclement campaign. Only Chou could have then found his way into the new supreme military council, chaired by the man he had opposed – Mao Tse-tung. Though criticized during the Cultural Revolution, he managed to survive and retain his political power within the CCP.

Chu Teh

One of China's great revolutionary soldiers. Born in Sichuan Province in December 1886, he died aged ninety in 1976. Chu Teh was one of the founders of the PLA and a senior Marshal of ten who were given the rank in September 1955. He was born into a poor peasant family, one of thirteen children. Chu Teh trained at the Yunnan Military Academy and later became involved with Sun Yat-sen's Nationalists. While in his early twenties Chu renounced his military life; women, gambling and opium took him over, until he joined the Communist Party in Berlin where he had already met that great diplomat of the future Chinese People's Republic, Chou Enlai. Chu Teh took part in the ill-fated Nanchang Uprising, later joining Mao at Jinggangshan where the Chinese Workers' and Peasants' Red Army was formed. Chu was their commander and Mao the political commissar. During the Sino-Japanese War, Chu commanded the Eighth Route Army.

Chu was promoted to be Commander-in-Chief of the Red Armies in 1930. Later in his career he became Vice-Chairman of the Party's Politburo and member of the Military Affairs Committee, along with other important appointments. During his time he led delegations to all parts of the world including Moscow, Hungary, Poland and Czechoslovakia.

Like many of Mao's associates during the Cultural Revolution, he was physically attacked by Red Guards.

Deng Xiaoping

As China's leader, Deng is also the Commander in Chief of the People's Liberation Army. He controls the military through his chairmanship of two important committees: the Central Military Commission and the Military Commission of the Chinese Communist Party's Central Committee. To safeguard his military and political policies, Deng has appointed trusted comrades to key defence posts.

Deng Xiaoping, born 1904 in Chiating, Sichuan Province, has attempted during his time in power to shed China's national Maoist straitjacket and introduce sweeping communist liberal reforms.

He joined the Communist Party in France and learned his Marxism from the five years he spent amongst French workers. Following a short stay in Russia he found his way to Jinggangshan and the Southern Jiangxi Soviet, joining the political department of the Red Army and editing *Red Star*, the army's propaganda newspaper. A Long March veteran, he became the political commissar of the Eighth Route Army and close associate of Liu Shaoqi. By 1953 his power and influence had increased and he was appointed acting Premier.

In 1966, although he was re-elected to the Politburo, where he ranked sixth in seniority, his political power was sharply curtailed. For some ten years Deng had little political influence. It was only in 1977 that he was able once again to assert himself in China's politics.

In recent months Deng has been plagued by internal power plays within the Party. Demonstrations by students and dissidents in several of China's cities have embarrassed Deng both inside and outside China. As a result of the worst rioting since the Cultural Revolution, political heads had to roll. But few Western observers anticipated that it would be Deng's long-time comrade Hu Yao-bang, Secretary General of the Chinese Communist Party, who would be forced to make the sacrifice and 'resign'.

At the Thirteenth Party Congress planned for late 1987, Deng, now eighty-three years old, is expected to step down. He will be remembered as a politically astute leader, a survivor who attempted to put Maoism behind him and launch China into an era of liberal modernization.

He Long

One of the great revolutionary fighters of the communist movement who at the age of fifty-nine became a Marshal of the People's Republic of China and was awarded three of the nation's highest military honours. He was born in 1896 in Sangchi County, Hunan Province, south of the Yangtze. Like many of his comrades, He Long was born into a poor peasant family, the only son of three children. As a young man he commanded a brigade in the KMT forces, then joined the Communist Party in 1926. Along with Chu Teh, he took part in the August 1 Nanchang Uprising; when it failed, he fled to Shanghai, and later commenced guerrilla activities in the Jiangxi-Hunan area. At the outset of his own 'March' he joined forces with Xiao Ke, a communist revolutionary ten years younger than himself who commanded the Sixth Red Army, and together they made their way to the north-western stronghold at Yan'an and Bao'an. In his political life he held senior positions: member of the Politburo, Minister of Physical Culture, and a Vice-Premier.

This great revolutionary soldier came to a cruel end during the Cultural Revolution. Even the strong relationship he had formed with Chou Enlai failed to save him. It is said that Lin Biao was responsible for He Long's murder.

A long time diabetic, He Long required regular insulin injections. As a prisoner of the Red Guards, the injections were changed to glucose. His was a humiliating death; he and his wife were confined in their courtyard without water during the hottest months of the year. A few hours before he died, He Long was taken away by his guards and his wife never saw him again.

Hu Yaobang

Former General Secretary of the Chinese Communist Party, the sprightly seventy-one year old Hu Yaobang is a recent victim of the renewed power struggle within the Chinese government. Hu is one of the highest ranking members of the party to be deposed since the Cultural Revolution. His demise can be attributed to the student riots in China's major cities during the latter part of 1986, and also to the fact that many of his political adversaries thought that Hu was becoming intoxicated with Western capitalism. He still retains his position in the Politburo and the Central Committee, but has been succeeded as General Secretary by another Dengist, Premier Zhao Ziyang.

Hunan-born Hu enlisted in the Red Army as a boy. During the Long March he was wounded during a KMT bombing raid, near Zunyi. He held political appointments in Sichuan and Shaanxi, and was nominated to the Politburo at the Eleventh Party Congress. A Deng protégé, Hu's political career appears to have followed the same turbulent, see-saw pattern as that of his mentor.

Jiang Qing

Mao's fourth wife and one-time Shanghai actress, she was born in Shandong Province in 1914. A political schemer, she edged her way from the stage door to the corridors of political power in Peking by way of the casting couch, and certainly saw herself becoming China's Communist Empress on Mao's death. As a member of the Gang of Four, a radical political group that tried to seize power after Mao died, she was arrested, convicted and given a suspended death sentence. She is still imprisoned, but there have been recent suggestions in the Chinese press that she could be released.

Lin Biao

An outstanding military commander and politician who was killed in mysterious circumstances. He was one of Mao's closest Comrades in Arms, and his chosen successor. There is little doubt that in 1971 Lin Biao was at the centre of a coup that went wrong. He fled to the Soviet Union, but his plane crashed and there were no known survivors. Accounts of the crash are various. Some say his Trident aircraft was shot down by pursuing fighters; others say there was shooting inside the aircraft before it crashed.

Lin Biao was born near Wuhan, Hubei Province in 1907. Like many of China's professional soldiers of the time, Lin, in his early years, was a member of the Kuomintang and trained at the Whampoa Military Academy. He became a Communist when Chiang Kai-shek ordered all military personnel to choose between the KMT and the Communist Party. It fell to Lin Biao, along with Peng Dehuai, to lead the breakout from Southern Jiangxi at the outset of the Long March. He was strongly influenced by the Soviet Union, and it is believed that he fought alongside Russian troops during the defence of Leningrad. During the War of Liberation his North-East Field Army overwhelmed the Nationalist forces until he finally controlled all of Manchuria. During 1955 he was made a Politburo member and a Marshal of the People's Republic. In 1959 he succeeded Peng Dehuai as Minister of Defence. When he died he was labelled a traitor of the state. In recent years Lin Biao's place in China's history is being re-evaluated.

Liu Shaoqi

Politician and Party organizer, Liu was born in 1898 in Hunan, the son of a well-to-do peasant family. Liu was regarded as a bland and colourless figure within the Party's political hierarchy; nevertheless, he had a strong influence upon and a following among his contemporaries. Like many of China's revolutionary leaders, he liked the good life; he certainly married three or four times. As a young man Liu was engaged in organizing communist cells, socialist youth groups and trade unions. He wrote *How to be a Good Communist* and *On Inner Party Struggle*. There are differing reports as to whether he took part in the Long March. Edgar Snow, in *Red Star over China*, states that Liu Shaoqi took part in the retreat from Southern Jiangxi, then departed to reorganize the Communist Party in the White areas of North China, making his headquarters in Peking and Tientsin. In due course he became Head of State.

But Liu was imprudent enough to criticize a number of Mao's political innovations; additionally, Mao's wife Jiang Qing disliked Liu's wife. Political power ebbed away from Liu, and he was reduced within the Politburo from second to eighth place. As the political power game continued, Liu was replaced by Lin Biao. During the Cultural Revolution he suffered at the hands of the notorious Red Guards. Virtually forgotten, he died an ignominious death in prison in 1969. He was rehabilitated in 1980.

Mao Tse-tung

He was known as the Great Helmsman of China's Communist revolution; his credo of freedom for the masses was tempered by a dictatorial wielding of power reminiscent of China's dynastic past. Mao was born in 1893 in Shaoshan, a small village in the southern province of Hunan.

The four-times-married Mao – his first wife was a child bride – was one of a family of four, three boys and an adopted girl. Mao does not appear to have come from a happy home; he was beaten by his father and schoolmaster, and like most children of the time was made to work in his father's fields. In today's vocabulary, Mao's father was an entrepreneur; from being a middle-class peasant, through various business transactions, he became a prosperous merchant.

Mao was a footloose youth; he taught a little, involved himself in writing political tracts, spent six months with the Republican Army at a nearby garrison, worked in a Shanghai laundry, and for a time was librarian and general factotum at the Peking University. Mao was obviously an intelligent youth with an inquisitive mind and social conscience. Along with his compulsive appetite for all things 'political', Mao felt that he must condition his body as efficiently as his mind. He walked a great deal without shoes and swam in icy water. It is interesting to note what Clare Hollingworth says of Mao in her book *Mao, and the Men against Him*:

> In 1918, Mao, at the age of twenty-five, appeared to have the educational attainments of an intelligent student of the period of around seventeen. Despite his wide reading, he knew little or

nothing about science, geography, economics or engineering. But the future Chairman had already realized he was a natural leader of men and developed the ambition to gain local political power. Mao at that time held views on life which were contradictory as they combined his conviction of personal superiority over the less well-educated workers with a strong determination not to adopt the manners or the vocabulary of the mandarin. Mao was constantly looking for a political doctrine that would enable the miserable lives of the peasants to be improved. Nevertheless, his strong Nationalist tendencies did not prevent him from wanting to import foreign books and political philosophies as well as technical innovations.

At the heart of Mao's revolutionary success was the belief that, with the enlisted help and political indoctrination of the peasant masses, he could attain all his political objectives for China. It was this Peasant Power that brought about the Chinese People's Republic, and Maoist Communism.

The personification of Peasant Power which gave Mao his strength was the Red Army – today's People's Liberation Army.

Mao was a founder member of the Chinese Communist Party. Following liberation and the proclamation of the People's Republic in 1949, Mao was State Chairman for ten years. He married his actress wife Jiang Qing in Yan'an in 1940.

A political tyrant as well as being one of the world's great revolutionaries, the Chairman of the Central Committee of the Communist Party of China died in Peking, some say from a combination of heart attacks and Parkinson's Disease, on September 9 1976.

Peng Dehuai

A formidable guerrilla fighter and commander who was highly regarded by all those who fought alongside him. Born in 1902 in Hunan Province, he ran away from home to join the army, and by the age of eighteen was a platoon commander; at twenty-five with the Kuomintang forces, he commanded a brigade. A leader of the peasant uprising in Hunan, he was one of the early revolutionary leaders to join Mao and Chu Teh in their rebel stronghold in Jinggangshan. During the Long March, he and his men formed the advance out of the Southern Jiangxi Soviet. During the time that Mao and his Communists were in the North-West, Peng Dehuai commanded the First Front Army. The world came to know about Peng during the Korean War; he commanded the Chinese People's Volunteers (CPVs) during this campaign. In 1955, he was created a Marshal of the People's Republic.

At the time when the Soviet Union was involved in the modernization of the PLA, Peng Dehuai acted as the liaison officer between the PLA and its Russian advisers. Like Liu Shaoqi, however, Peng was a man who criticized Mao with fatal consequences. Following the humiliation of China's force in Korea, he was convinced that China needed Russian help in retraining and equipping the PLA. Mao, on the other hand, felt that since their guerrilla armies and tactics had succeeded in the past, they could withstand anything in the future. After becoming Minister of Defence, Peng was dismissed in 1959, another victim of Mao's irrational temperament and inflexible reasoning. Whatever the cause of Peng's dismissal, his PLA fighters and comrades never forgot him.

Dr Sun Yat-sen

Although Dr Sun Yat-sen, as founder of the KMT, can be regarded as the father of China's Republican movement, becoming the country's first President, his claim to political power and the Presidency was always a fragile one.

Born into a poor farming family in Guangdong Province in 1866, he somehow managed to train as a doctor. Like many of China's leaders, Sun was a member of a secret society – the Hsing Chung Hui – whose sole aim was the overthrow of the Manchu Government. Sun's early political career nearly came to an end in London, England. It is reported that he was kidnapped by Chinese agents who had every intention of taking him back to China for execution. It was due to the intervention of Lord Salisbury, the Prime Minister of the day, that Sun Yat-sen was freed. And on December 29 1911 he became the first – albeit in a provisional capacity – President of the new Republic. Constant pressure, however, from China's warlords prevented Sun from establishing any real political power.

Sun came to know Chiang Kai-shek in Japan, and appointed him to organize the training of China's Kuomintang Nationalist Army. Western support for Sun's revolutionary movement never materialized; in desperation he turned to the Soviets, who gave him money and political 'guidance' in the form of their two agents, Adolf Joffe and Michael Borodin. From that time Sun always looked to the Soviet Union as the model on which China was to ultimately obtain her liberation from Imperialism.

1 China's Dynastic Past

Of all the world's civilizations China, with its rigidly hierarchical society, rich in the arts, science and philosophy, is for Westerners a particularly enigmatic and baffling land.

The plough and the wheelbarrow were invented in China. The crossbow, gunpowder, stirrups, paper and printing, the arcuballistae – a formidable ancient weapon that released arrows in a powerful barrage – herbal medicine, exotic glazed pottery, all these and much else find their origins in China's past.

In some ways the development of China may be regarded as the very mirror of humankind: birth, growth, conflict, poverty, conquest, learning, intrigue, power and riches, all these stages can be seen in the unfolding of China's history.

Possibly it is because men and women have a need to see themselves at the beginning of their half-a-million-year-long journey, and to identify their cultural roots at a particular point in time, that most of us are drawn to all things Chinese. China and the West are divided by immense differences of culture and social evolution, but nevertheless we are always eager to explore her past, to understand her present and to speculate upon her future.

Archaeologists in China have uncovered fossilized human remains going back 600,000 years. Relics of the 500,000-year-old Peking Man were found at Zhoukoudian, to the South of Peking, in the 1920s. Unfortunately much of the stone and bronze age material, the evidence of early civilization which was unearthed during the Sino-Japanese War, is now lost.

It is in Northern China, along the valleys and waterways of the Wei and Yellow Rivers, that the earliest remains of Chinese civilization are to be found. In these early agricultural river communities archaeologists have discovered early forms of writing: arranged characters and simple pictures, which have become known as pictograms.

Following China's prehistoric period, the dynastic progression is well documented, beginning with the Xia Dynasty c 2000 BC, and ending with the Qing in 1911 AD. A popular insurrection saw the end of the Xia Dynasty and ushered in the Shang. These were cultures that worked in bronze and cultivated wheat. At the turn of the century, archaeologists working at the site of the ancient city of Anyang, Henan Province, found evidence of the Shang between c 1750–1100 BC. The royal palace at Anyang was a structure of great beauty and grandeur and elaborate works of art were unearthed. There is also evidence that this was a barbaric society, practising animal and human sacrifice. Records show, furthermore, that there were trading links with the West. Whatever the foreign connections, however, the Shang seem to have retained the purity of their culture by means of the rigid isolationism which was to be so much a part of future Chinese society.

Following the Shang, the Zhou Dynasty was the longest in China's history, and did not start to decline until the fourth and third centuries BC. Thereafter, as a result of growing conflicts between local feudal rulers, China entered the era known as the Warring States Period (c 403–221 BC). Yet, in spite of the continuous wars during this time, this period is now viewed as a classical age, for a definite pattern to Chinese life emerged, shaped by the Confucian virtues of a benevolent monarchy, pacifism, justice, and personal loyalty. Both Confucian and Taoist philosophies have exerted great influence throughout China's more recent history. Confucius, a philosopher and teacher of ethics, extolled high moral values and respect for the family, the state, and the emperor. Taoism developed after Confucianism and advocated an honest, simple life, without interfering with the natural course of events. The two philosophies coexisted very successfully: in their professional lives the Chinese applied Confucianism, while within the family Taoist thought prevailed. Even as early as the Zhou period, however, we see developing the Son of Heaven doctrine, which gave subjects the right of rebellion against tyranni-cal monarchs and leaders, and thus provided moral justification for political conflict, and even revolution.

The next dynasty, the Qin, was short-lived (c 221–206 BC), but although it lasted only fifteen years it was a period of dramatic change. For the first time in China's history there was unity under one ruler, Qin Shi Huangdi, the First Emperor of Qin. In fact, it is to Emperor Qin's name that the westernized word 'China' is attri-buted. The First Emperor was ruthless and dictatorial: land-owners were deprived of their possessions, books were destroyed, and the helpless villagers were put to work on China's Great Wall, a defensive barrier which was completed by joining together the walls of communities along the northern border. Nevertheless, historians believe that it was during the brief dynasty of the Qin that the foundations of what was to become the Chinese Empire were laid.

Then, with the four-hundred-year-long Han Dynasty (c 206 BC–220 AD), came prosperity and expansion. Buddhism now appeared in Chinese society from India by way of the silk routes. Confucian teachings were integrated into a flourishing educational system, and this became the source material for the world's earliest institutionalized Civil Service. And the Han, unlike their predecessors, did not disappear beneath the dusts of time: they still survive in present-day China as the country's principal national grouping.

Feudal China developed four distinct strata of society: the *Shih, Nung, Kung,* and *Shang* – respectively, scholars and administrators, peasant farmers forming the core of society, craftsmen, and finally merchants. Intellectualism and creativity were more highly regarded in Imperial China than the pursuit of trade and barter.

The tenth century AD saw the establishment of the sophisticated Song Dynasty, poetry-loving, rich in artistic development, and with a fully-developed state bureaucracy. This was overthrown in 1211, when the Mongol cavalry of Genghis Khan swept across the Great Wall. Genghis established a new dynasty in 1279, the Yuan, and decided upon Peking as his capital. The city was ideally located, sufficiently central to control not only China but also the Mongolian Empire which extended beyond the Yellow River as far as the Danube.

Kublai Khan, grandson of the great Genghis, united China for the first time under an alien ruler, and became the first Yuan Emperor. The Mongols had little confidence in Chinese integrity, and they kept all political power within their own community. In consequence, the Chinese retreated within themselves, taking refuge in the arts and philosophy. It was at this time that the increased social stability and safety of travel established by the Mongols enabled foreign merchants, travellers and scholars, such as Marco Polo, to make their way into China, returning to Europe with scientific and artistic treasures.

Of all the Chinese dynasties, perhaps the Ming, successor to the Yuan, is the one with which the Western world is best acquainted, for it was the Ming who produced the delicate blue-and-white porcelain first known as chinaware. Also, it was into this period of severe imperial power, enforced by merciless punishment and frequent public executions, that the first Jesuit missionaries arrived. Maritime exploration now became of importance to the Chinese also, and fleets of their ships navigated the Indian Ocean to trade with India and Africa.

Nanking was the early Ming capital, but during the reign of the Emperor Yong Le this was transferred to Peking. Emperor Yong Le was a man of vision who wished to preserve the splendours of the Ming Dynasty. He began refurbishing the Great Wall and the Forbidden City, ransacked and in ruins from successive wars, was restored to its original magnificence.

Sadly the glorious dynasty of the Ming ended in ignominy during the seventeenth century. Weakened by famine, China was invaded for the second time by northern foreigners. Manchu tribesmen crossed the Great Wall and the dispirited Ming armies capitulated, allowing the enemy to enter Peking almost unopposed. Shamed by defeat, the last Ming Emperor hanged himself on Coal Hill, overlooking the golden tiled Forbidden City.

The expansionist Qing ruled over the largest empire in China's history, extending westwards well into Tibet, and north-east beyond Peking to the Russian border. The Manchu was to retain power until 1911. But with the arrival of Western traders, among the earliest of whom were the Portuguese who occupied Macau during the middle of the sixteenth century, China was to change dramatically, and the collapse of the Qing Dynasty would eventually be brought about by two factors: the unprincipled greed of

Chinese workers hauling boats on the Qiantang River. The hopeless conditions of the workers and peasants contributed to the endless turmoil and political confrontation in China.

the Western nations in their trade with China, and the introspective isolationism of the Qing government.

Emerging from the Dynastic Period we can see the characteristics of China's eventual national identity. The changing dynasties had brought periods of intense conflict and turmoil, alternating with developments in science, the arts, philosophy, and the legal code. Throughout China's turbulent history successive invaders had clearly failed to subjugate the Chinese: the conquerors would prevail for a time, then would gradually be absorbed into China's resilient and superior culture.

Although China's enemies had in the past invaded overland from the North, in the eighteenth and nineteenth centuries they entered China using a far easier route — by way of the sea, in brigantines and merchant clipper ships. Europe, mainly Britain, France and Holland, and later the United States, was now aware that there were rich pickings of silk and tea to be obtained from trading around the China Seas. As the self-sufficient Chinese required nothing from these Western traders, all goods were paid for in silver. At first the Manchus were able to control the flow of trade with the West by limiting commerce to the ports of Canton and Macau. Foreign traders were confined to the waterfronts, and business was conducted solely through a group of authorized Chinese merchants — later to become known as Hongs.

But European traders, in particular the British, were far from satisfied at being thus restricted, and gradually overcame the Manchus' resistance to wider trading rights. Then, frustrated at having little to sell that the Chinese needed, the British — to their lasting shame — together with the other European traders introduced a product from India to remedy this lack: opium. The last Manchu Emperor made desperate attempts to end this despicable commerce, but he was too late — with the collaboration of corrupt Chinese officials, opium addiction had taken hold of the Empire. After four opium wars, the final one of which ended in 1860, the commercial European invasion of China was complete.

Elsewhere, territorial incursions into the Chinese Empire took place: the French appropriated much of Cochin China, the Russians took over part of Siberia, east of the Amur River, and Taiwan was absorbed by the Japanese.

During the latter part of the nineteenth century, a radical Christian sect tried to invigorate the decaying Manchu Dynasty. The Taiping Rebellion was a brave attempt by a Christian zealot, Hong Xiuquan, to restore traditional values and morals in his country by means of Christian teachings. Today the acceptance of

Naked workers mining and transporting coal during the early part of the century. Working in such conditions, the Chinese workers stored up bitterness and resentment towards their employers and landlords. Here was the breeding ground for Mao's revolution.

these doctrines of love and equality is regarded by many as the beginning of twentieth-century communist reforms. Over a ten year period Hong Xiuquan had gathered a half-a-million-strong Christian movement around himself, influencing a large part of Southern China. Here was a reform movement strong enough to be a counterforce to the dynastic tradition. The Taiping Rebellion, with its theories of tax reforms and the public ownership of land, was a movement which had wide popular appeal, especially among the peasant farmers. The Taiping also condemned opium, tobacco, foot binding, arranged marriages and prostitution. In spite of this, as a reforming faction it failed. Twenty million people are reported to have been killed during the uprising, which was brutally put down by the ailing Qing government, supported by Western forces.

At the turn of the century, therefore, China was once again a society in disruption. The European powers were thus able to gain access to most of the remaining ports they needed for trading along China's coast, and it was at this time that Britain acquired Hong Kong. Western embassies were established in Peking, and representatives from major European companies, together with missionaries, made their way into China's remoter provinces, such as Hubei and Sichuan.

Once again, the poverty and suffering of the peasants brought about a further uprising, one of the most widely-reported of that time – the Boxer Rebellion. The Boxers, one of China's many secret societies, discreetly joined forces with the Manchu government in an attempt to expel all aliens from the country. In the winter of 1899 the foreign legations' compound in Peking was laid under siege for fifty-five days. Many people, Chinese as well as European, died during the rebellion. Finally, however, the legations were relieved by an eight-nation expeditionary force, during which operation the Manchus transferred their imperial court from Peking to Xian, remaining there until 1902.

Six years later, in 1908, the Empress Dowager Ci Xi, who had led the collusion with the Boxers during the rebellion, died and the final days of the Manchu Empire came under the authority of the two-year-old child, Emperor Puyi, and his advisers. This figure-head ruler, the last of the 'Imperial Sons of Heaven', was used by successive powers in China, both revolutionary and foreign. At first he was allowed to maintain his court in the Forbidden City, with the full trappings of imperial life. Later he was obliged to seek refuge with the Japanese, who made him a symbolic Head of State, the Puppet Emperor of Manchuria. When the Communists came to power they imprisoned him and, following a ten year rectification period, he was made the gardener in Peking's Botanical Gardens. He died of cancer just twenty years ago in 1967, the last mortal reminder of China's imperial past. Four thousand years of dynastic rule had ended.

2 The Birth of Nationalism and Communism

The Republican movement can be looked upon as the forerunner to the formation of the Communist State, which propelled China into the second half of the twentieth century. Republicanism was the great divide: thenceforward, Chinese society was irrevocably set on the path to change.

It was the son of a peasant, Dr Sun Yat-sen, a Christian convert and a medical practitioner, who brought into being fragile Republican China in 1912 and established his provisional form of government in the southern city of Nanking. Though born in Guangdong Province, he had lived for a time in Japan, then travelled to Europe and America, enlisting support for China's reforms, and in consequence many regarded Sun Yat-sen as an 'Overseas Chinese' – a reproachful comment. There were those in the nationalist movement who resented his leadership, and his government in Nanking was short-lived. Together with its founding members, he was forced into exile following the assassination of the leader of the Republican Party, Sung Chiao-jen.

A power vacuum was then created; in Peking the Manchus had abdicated their imperial power and installed Yuan Shikai, one of the Empress' former generals, as provisional President. Yuan Shikai, who also appeared to have the confidence of the foreign community, had firm dictatorial objectives; and without doubt saw himself not only as political leader, but as the new Emperor of China, creating another dynastic line. When the Japanese thwarted his aspirations, in conjunction with his own rebellious generals, the concept of a new dynasty was conclusively laid to rest, never again to be resurrected. Yuan Shikai died, of ill-health, while Europe was at war, in 1916. Now China was to be exposed to further internal conflicts, in a period known as the Warlord Era.

Some scholars claim that China's history and development has a definite recurring pattern and that careful analysis of Chinese political winds will reveal the underlying purpose and direction of events like these. The ten year Warlord period falls into that familiar historical pattern: civic and political confusion after the end of one great dynasty, followed by the creation of another.

With no central government or political figure to unite the country, the militarists took over. It was a lawless period; the powerful warlords extracted riches at will, at the expense of the people and the country. Dozens of small armies came into being and the population was terrorized and exploited. Once they had accumulated a sufficient fortune, the warlords would retreat to the safety of one of the many international settlements, allowing others to take their place. China was suffering from an internal political and economic haemorrhage, and conditions for revolution were already emerging.

Dr Sun's Nationalist Party, the Kuomintang, still had a power base in the South. However, the West preferred to negotiate with whichever warlord was resident in Peking. Thus it was Russia and the Bolshevik Revolution that influenced Sun Yat-sen, and it was the Soviet system that became China's path to Communism.

Following the Great War (1914–8), the Chinese resented the outcome of the Versailles Peace Conference, since it gave former German concessions in Shandong to Japan. Student demonstrations spread from the university at Peking to other major centres. A strong xenophobic movement swept through the country, involving all social levels: peasant, student, landowner and intellectual.

These civil disorders later became known as the Fourth of May Uprising (1919), a date commemorated by the Communist Party to this day as an historic event in China's political evolution. The May 4 Movement is also seen as expressing the Chinese people's fundamental desire for national unity and self-determination. National fervency had overcome mere republican idealism, and in 1921 the Chinese Communist Party was born in the French Concession at Shanghai – a city, which, in contrast to the stodgy political society of Peking, has always been associated with cultural progressiveness and reforming ideas. Among its early members was a young man from the Communist cell in Hunan, about whom the world was to hear a great deal in the years ahead – Mao Tse-tung.

Meanwhile the foreign residents, comfortably lodged in their settlements, were for the most part oblivious to China's internal changes and unsuspecting of the impending revolution that was about to shatter their cosy colonialist world. After obtaining Russian assurances that they would support his authority, Dr Sun returned from exile to his base in Southern China. Although his Nationalists had failed over the years to consolidate a firm political platform, they now re-emerged and made another determined attempt to unify China, on this occasion by joining forces with the

Mao Tse-tung, the young
revolutionary.

Communists, who were allowed individually to become members
of the Kuomintang. It was an uneasy alliance, certainly as far as
Sun Yat-sen was concerned, but one which his new-found Soviet
advisers encouraged.

Sun was by this time fully committed to Marxist-Leninist
thinking, disillusioned after years of believing in Western democ-
racy, which now, and during his earlier efforts to establish a
democratic China, he felt had deserted him in his hour of need. To
strengthen his power base, the Russians assisted him by establishing a military academy at Whampoa in Canton. At its head Sun
appointed two promising young men, one a militarist, the other a
young emerging revolutionary – their names: Chiang Kai-shek and
Chou Enlai.

Sun was an idealist, a man who fought for a unified China, free

of all forms of foreign exploitation and intervention. He never realized his ambition. China was still a divided nation when he died, aged fifty-nine, in March 1925.

By 1926, however, Chiang Kai-shek had put together his Nationalist forces and mounted a joint Nationalist/Communist military campaign – the Northern Expedition 1926-7 – in a final attempt to bring about a united China. It was a two-pronged attack on the southern warlords, one led by himself as overall Commander in Chief of the Nationalist Forces, the other led by Tang Shengzhi.

As Chiang Kai-shek's forces pushed northwards towards the city of Nanchang on their way to capture Nanking and Shanghai, Tang Shengzhi overcame the city of Wuhan, the future seat of Nationalist government. Meanwhile the Communists and the extreme left of the Kuomintang were organizing the peasant population against the landowners. The tenuous alliance between Chiang and the Communists was about to end. As the Kuomintang

Few weapons were available to the early peasant revolutionaries. In 1926, prior to the establishment of the Red Army, a peasant spear corps was founded.

forces overcame Nanking and Shanghai, in an ultimate bid for supreme power, Chiang decided the time had come to eliminate the Communist dissenters within his ranks. Without warning, his forces executed thousands of Communists and their sympathizers in Shanghai. There were similar killings in Canton, Changsha and Nanchang. One of China's future political leaders, Chou Enlai, narrowly escaped execution during these massacres.

Several differing accounts exist of Chou's escape, but the event is recalled with convincing realism in Harrison Salisbury's book, *The Long March*.

> On the day after the massacre, Chou, accompanied by his six bodyguards and Gu Shunzhang, went to the Second Division of the Twenty-Sixth Army. The Army was commanded by General Bai Chongxi. The Second Division was charged with 'restoring order' and was disarming the workers' militia. Chou knew that there were communists and communist sympathizers among the officers of the Division, and he and Gu went to protest about what was going on. Immediately they and the bodyguards were disarmed and put under detention. The Chief of the Division, Zhao Shu – a KMT political commissar who was sympathetic to the communists and whose daughter was a Party Member – was not there. Chou was received by the Deputy Commander Si Lie, who was thought to be friendly. His younger brother was an underground Party Member and had been an assistant to Chou at the Whampoa Academy. But Sie Lie was hostile. The argument grew heated, and it was plain that he had no intention of letting Chou go. Finally, Zhao Shu, the political commissar arrived. They drew Si Lie into an adjoining room. Heated words

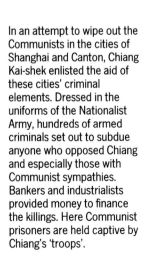

In an attempt to wipe out the Communists in the cities of Shanghai and Canton, Chiang Kai-shek enlisted the aid of these cities' criminal elements. Dressed in the uniforms of the Nationalist Army, hundreds of armed criminals set out to subdue anyone who opposed Chiang and especially those with Communist sympathies. Bankers and industrialists provided money to finance the killings. Here Communist prisoners are held captive by Chiang's 'troops'.

could be heard. Presently the pair emerged, apologized to Chou Enlai, restored the arms and let everyone go. Chou reported to Party Headquarters what had happened, then slipped away to Wuhan. But for the intervention of the political commissar, Chou's career, like that of so many fellow communists, probably would have come to a bloody end.

The Red Army, at first known as the National Revolutionary Army, forerunner of the People's Liberation Army, grew out of the peasant Nanchang Uprising on August 1 1927. Although it was unsuccessful, it is dear to the hearts of China's militarists; their badges and uniform buttons (insignia) bear the Chinese character *bei yi*, meaning eight-one – the eighth month and the first day, the date of the abortive uprising.

Nanchang was chosen for insurrection for a specific reason; unknown to any save one or two high-ranking members of the Party, the Communists had a highly-placed 'mole' in the local Nationalist forces. He was the Chief of Security, Chu Teh, who would become one of the Red Army's most outstanding generals. At the time of the uprising, Chu had been a Communist for some five years, following nomination into the Party by Chou Enlai in Berlin, and he was to be elected the Red Army's Commander in Chief – a title he retained until after the establishment of the People's Republic in 1949.

By all accounts the uprising would have had every chance of success, had not the Communists placed too much confidence in obtaining the co-operation of the Nationalist Commander of the Second Front Army, General Zhang Fakui. Led by Chu Teh, the rebels took Nanchang with ease – but they could not hold it. Within days Zhang Fakui's Nationalist Second Front Army was pushing them south. The newly-founded Red Army was suffering its first defeat and was on the run. It retreated south to Swatow in Guangdong Province but again failed to hold a position and was pushed even further south. Now desperate to secure a firm base from which they could operate, the rebels tried to secure Canton while an internal putsch was in progress. Again they were overcome by superior KMT Forces, and forced to retreat once more.

Slipping through the Nationalist lines, their morale low, the rebels made their way north into Southern Hunan, and eventually joined forces with Mao Tse-tung, who had established his headquarters in the region. It was in this remote wilderness area, the first rural Soviet in China, on the borders of Hunan and Jiangxi, that Mao and Chu Teh formed the basis of a military partnership that was to bring about the revolution from which the People's Republic

An early photograph of Chou Enlai. He was one of the founding members of the Communist Youth League in 1920–1. A highly respected diplomat, he eventually became Prime Minister and Foreign Minister of the People's Republic of China.

of China emerged twenty-one years later, on October 1 1949.

Notwithstanding the Churchillian notion that a military retreat brings few benefits, the Nanchang Uprising did have certain positive elements. At the time of the rebellion there emerged some of the outstanding figures who were to form the foundations of the New China: leaders such as Chou Enlai, the brilliant military tactician Chu Teh, and 'fighters' who were later to become Marshals: Chen Yi, He Long, Liu Bocheng, Lin Biao and Nie Rongzhen, now Vice-Chairman of the Party's Military Commission and close friend of Deng Xiaoping.

During its time in Hunan, and later in Southern Jiangxi, the Red Army consolidated its political ideals and perfected its military training, thus creating a highly disciplined army of guerrilla fighters. The original small force which had arrived at its mountain stronghold quickly grew, with additional guerrilla forces led by Chu Teh and Peng Dehuai.

It was during the early years at Jinggangshan in Southern Hunan that Mao expounded his theories for the peasant rebellion. In total contrast to the Marxist doctrine that revolution should begin with the urban working classes, Mao maintained that China's revolution could only succeed with the help of an enlightened and educated peasantry, who would supply food, shelter and man-power for his guerrilla armies. Since Karl Marx had maintained that peasants alone could hardly be a force to sustain a revolution, Mao's theory was far from popular with certain of China's Communists. Much to their surprise, however, the peasant move-ment prospered and spread. Some years later Mao explained China's political change in the following way:

> The ruthless economic exploitation and political oppression of the peasants by the landlord class forced them into numerous uprisings against its rule . . . It was the class struggle of the peasants, the peasant uprisings and peasant wars, that constituted the real motive force of historical development in Chinese feudal society. [1939]

Basically, Mao turned the ancient Chinese social strata upside down. The peasants, *Nung*, moved to the top, and below them in descending order were *Kung*, *Shih*, and *Shang* – artisans, scholars, and merchants.

To ensure discipline and strengthen co-operation with the peasants, the Red Army instituted simple rules of conduct: obey all orders promptly; confiscate nothing whatever from the poor peasantry; deliver directly to the government, for its disposal, all goods confiscated from landlords; replace all doors when you leave a house; return and roll up the straw matting on which you sleep; be courteous and polite to the people and help them when you can;

return all borrowed articles; be honest in all transactions with peasants; pay for all articles purchased; be sanitary and, especially, establish latrines a safe distance from people's houses. Over the years these rules have served them well in many campaigns, and to this day this is still the code of conduct expected from a fighter in the People's Liberation Army.

During their seven-year stay in the Jiangxi-Hunan border region, the Red Army's numbers steadily increased. Between 1931 and 1932 several contingents of the KMT forces defected to the peasant cause. By now Chiang Kai-shek was fully aware of a growing danger from the Red Army, and in 1934 he mounted a major offensive to deal with it. He had previously underestimated the determination and idealism of the rebels; several efforts to dislodge them from their mountain stronghold failed, and his fleeing troops left behind them arms to contribute to the Communists' supplies. The Red partisans' guerrilla tactics overcame every attempt to subdue them. The rebels had four simple guidelines for conducting their campaigns: when the enemy advances, we retreat; when the enemy halts and encamps, we harass him; when the enemy seeks to avoid a battle, we attack; when the enemy retreats, we pursue. Simple as these tactics were, by their implementation the Red Army was able to inflict heavy losses on Chiang Kai-shek's numerically superior and better equipped forces. Conversely, when the Red Army decided to abandon them and take up firm defensive positions against the major attack Chiang mounted on the advice of his German military advisers, the KMT overwhelmed them.

It has to be said, however, that although Mao always claimed in later years that the wrong tactics were used to counter Chiang's onslaught, it is doubtful if even the Red Army's well-proven guerrilla strategies would have prevailed against such staggering odds as the KMT forces represented at that time.

The military situation for what became known as the First Front Army, the Red Army and its followers in Southern Jiangxi, had seriously deteriorated: now they must either retreat or fight where they stood and be annihilated. The revolutionaries chose retreat, and preparations were begun for what in time would come to be known as the Long March.

3 The Long March

As the Red Army made their first faltering steps on that historic trek more than fifty years ago, few could have realized that they were treading the stony path of eventual nationhood. The march was at the same time a military retreat – an escape from the tragic reality of brother slaughtering brother – and a major and profoundly significant Communist migration. It occurred only just in time, for the Kuomintang Forces were closing in fast. Chiang's German advisers, Generals von Falkenhausen and Seeckt, had sensed victory and were urging him to move in his Kuomintang troops at once and finish off the Communists. Surrounded, the Red Army broke out from the ring of concrete bunkers the Nationalists had built around them, and fought their way westwards taking with them all the impedimenta of Government.

The Red Army fighters were in high spirits. After seemingly endless preparation, at last they were leaving. Creeping under cover of darkness, the 86,829 Communist soldiers, more than half of whom were fledgling recruits with little battle experience, slipped silently from their mountain encampment in Southern Jiangxi. Few, even among their leaders, knew where they were going. It was a time for escape and survival. Most of them, in fact, would fall and die by the wayside during the journey.

Each fighter carried sixty-five pounds of equipment; if his company had sufficient weapons, he would have a rifle or light machine-gun and one hundred cartridges. He would also have two grenades, and padded clothing as protection against the severe winter. Compared to some guerrilla armies, his force was well-armed, with more than thirty thousand rifles and light automatic weapons, thirty-eight mortars and a few light field guns. Ammunition stocks consisted of 1,801,640 cartridges, 2,523 mortar shells, and over 76,000 grenades. Two aircraft captured from the Nationalists' large air force turned out to be of little use, since there was insufficient petrol to keep them airborne.

There must have been great sadness among the families left behind as the troops pulled out. Southern Jiangxi had been their

The early revolutionaries – the forerunners of the Red Army and the PLA – made their base on the mountains on the Hunan Jiangxi border. As the fledgling peasant army increased in number, food supplies in the small Jinggangshan base became a problem so the five thousand strong revolutionary army moved its base to Yudu and Ruijin in Southern Jiangxi. This historic photograph shows the straggling peasant army at the outset of the Long March.

home for many years; they had tamed the land, subdued greedy landowners and warlords, sons and daughters had been born there. No one was exempt from sorrow: all children were left behind with peasant families. Even He Zizhen, Mao's wife, was forced to forsake her two children, never to see them again. The army was only doing what other armies had done in the past. Nevertheless, there is a callousness about any army that deserts its sick, wounded and loved ones, an inhumanity that can only be justified by the hopelessness of the situation in which the Communists found themselves.

They set out on the night of October 16 1934, their average age just nineteen. Few women accompanied the main body of the marchers: the thirty or so women who did so were wives of the leaders, cadres or nursing orderlies.

There appears to have been strict rules affecting husband and wife relationships during the march. Whether it was believed that marital cohabitation would affect morale and fighting efficiency when there were so few women, it is difficult to say. Had the Red Army, on the other hand, encouraged the principle of camp followers, which has prevailed in numerous armies down the ages, the case for marital abstinence would have been redundant. Perhaps the revolutionary zeal and fervour of the Communists also bred a kind of puritanical ingenuousness; even today, there are signs of a pronounced puritanical attitude existing between the sexes within the PLA.

At about the time when the unwieldy formation of the Red Army was making its way across the incompleted Canton-Wuhan railway, *The Times* in London, on page eleven of their October 27 edition, printed a three-inch story from their correspondent in Hong Kong. Nationalist troops from Canton, it reported, were being sent to the Kiangsi (Jiangxi) border region where there had been severe fighting. It was believed that the KMT forces had the upper hand, and that the Reds were being bombed by sixty Nationalist aircraft. The story went on to say that Mrs Bosshardt and Mrs Haymans, the wives of two missionaries, had been released by Communist bandits in order to carry a demand for the ransom of their husbands. The women said that the Communists stole everything they could lay their hands on.

In fact, the Communists were hoping to raise as much as $700,000 in ransom money, which would help to finance their war effort. Thus Rudolf Bosshardt and Arnolis Haymans, of the China Inland Mission, were among the few foreign observers to acquire first-hand knowledge of the Red Army at the time of the Long March. During their captivity they made a futile attempt at escape and were lucky to avoid execution. Bosshardt managed to ingratiate himself with his captors by crocheting garments for the troops. They were prisoners of the Reds for more than a year, and on their release Haymans was ransomed for ten thousand silver dollars. Bosshardt was given his freedom without paying a penny.

In October 1934 momentous events were taking place. The world was changing. The newspapers of the time, however, regarded China as having very little news value. Instead, they reported the Lindbergh case, church strife in Germany, and a fresh attempt on the Melbourne to London flying record by Cathcart Jones and Waller, in the de Havilland Comet. Their machine, they said, was splendid and they were confident of breaking the record. It was reported that the fliers were averaging 228 miles per hour.

From time to time theorists have debated whether the Long March began as a sudden and ignominious retreat, or was a well-planned piece of military strategy. There are numerous aspects of the March which remain unexplained to this day; even the Chinese and the few surviving octogenarian marchers regard the official narrative as containing many contradictions and uncertainties. It would appear, from what evidence there is, that the march was a planned retreat, though at times it was casual and unpredictable. Some accounts tell us that preparations were in progress during the summer of 1934, six months before the eventual departure.

At that time recruits were urgently needed by the Red Army's commanders, for heavy losses had been sustained fighting off the encircling Nationalist armies. So throughout the Southern Jiangxi area, a recruiting drive was initiated; as recruits came mainly from peasant families, their relatives would receive tax advantages and help with their crops. Harrison Salisbury, author of *The Long March*, speaking about the expansion of the Red Army prior to the Long March gives this interesting account:

> The extraordinary recruiting drive of spring and summer 1934, was an integral part of this plan to build back the Red Army's strength to mobilize all available manpower in the Jiangxi area. A parallel campaign was launched to collect foodstuffs: heavier requisitions were ordered; the peasants were appealed to for contributions. There

When the Red Army set out on their Long March from Southern Jiangxi, they took with them all the trappings of government, printing presses, silver for coin-making, sewing machines for uniforms and costumes for their travelling theatre group. Here young actors in the opera group of the Red Army rehearse a dance routine.

was a drive for loans. More silver dollars were struck. Winter clothing was made. Workshops began repairing guns and weapons. New grenades were turned out. Old battlefields were scoured for spent cartridges. The brass cases were refilled with powder and lead. When lead ran out, wooden heads were whittled. A propaganda drive was launched to get peasant women to make straw sandals for the soldiers. Sandals wore out rapidly. Soldiers tried to start a march with a couple of pairs in their knapsacks. The women were told to make the new sandals of extra thickness, a certain hint of a long march.

In view of all this, it is difficult to understand why the Nationalists' intelligence was so inadequate and failed to anticipate the Communists' withdrawal.

There are some Chinese commentators who are still bewildered by various Red Army troop movements during the summer of 1934, prior to the main breakout in the autumn. The Nationalists were by this time moving in on the Soviet areas, and their blockade was having a damaging effect. The first of these unexplained movements was undertaken by the Seventh and Tenth Red Armies – some ten thousand fighters in all – who attempted to move westwards out of Fujian Province into neighbouring Jiangxi. Some say it was a propaganda manoeuvre to entice Nationalist troops to the Red cause. If it was a diversion intended to test the strength of the enemy, it failed. Basically it was poor military strategy. Kuomintang forces tore the two armies apart. The few survivors melted into the surrounding countryside and fought as guerrilla bands, in time finding their way to the new Fourth Army.

Xiao Ke, commanding the Sixth Red Army on the Guangdong-Hunan border area, made a similar breakout in August 1934. Following numerous skirmishes with the enemy, he linked up with He Long's Second Army in Northern Hunan several weeks later. He paid a heavy price both in men and materials. Out of a fighting force of nine thousand, only four thousand reached their destination. In time their joint armies – now the Second Front Army – would also make their own march, first south into Guizhou and Yunan in the shadow of the Tibetan ranges, then north crossing the Golden Sands River and the Great Snowy Mountains to the headquarters of Zhang Guotao's Fourth Front Army at Garze in North-Western Sichuan.

It must be remembered that there was not one, but several armies of retreating Red fighters. Although the principal Communist base was at Yudu and Ruijin in Southern Jiangxi, there were others. Often called Rural Soviets, these somewhat smaller communist enclaves were to be found in Hunan, Hubei, Fujian, Henan and Sichuan. But the 'Mother House' of Chinese Communism and the spiritual heart of the revolution was in Southern Jiangxi. It was also the home of many of China's future leaders; men like Chou Enlai, Nie Rongzhen, Lin Biao, Chen Yi and Peng Dehuai; men who were to become the architects of a new China.

When the First Front Army with its six-mile-long body of marchers struck out on its fighting retreat from Southern Jiangxi during that bleak October night in 1934, their first objective was to join up with He Long's Second Front Army in Northern Hunan. Even the leaders were unaware that their plans and route were to change many times in the months ahead. Two army groups, commanded by the veteran guerrilla fighters Lin Biao and Peng Dehuai, prepared the way ahead, acting as vanguard to the main column of marchers. Every single fighter knew he was engaging in a fight to the finish: these peasant guerrillas had nothing to lose and everything to gain. A nation of justice and equality was their Promised Land, and they were prepared to die for it.

'Red Bandits' was a name frequently given to the Red Army's soldiers by Western newspapers of the day. However, although there certainly were former members of bandit gangs and warlord armies in their ranks, for the most part a fighter was from peasant stock. Nevertheless, once he had served with his unit for a reasonable period of time, he was far superior in the field to any warlord army gunman. His superiority lay in the sound leadership he received, discipline and well-understood ideological objectives. Everyone, from fighter to high-ranking cadre, was totally committed to the revolutionary cause. Like Cromwell's Ironsides, they were trained to know what they fought for and to love what they knew. As a peasant agrarian army, they were able to withstand endless hardship. Near monastic in their living, they ate and drank the simplest fare: cabbage, millet, meat and hot water, as unboiled water was likely to be contaminated.

According to Edgar Snow, one of the few writers who managed to gain a daily insight into the Red Army of this period, a soldier, even when not fighting, would have a full and busy day. If not involved in some garrison duty or other he would work a six day week, beginning at 5.00 am with exercises followed by breakfast. During the morning he would drill and be lectured in politics, with study and sports periods after lunch and the day would finish with a meal, songs and group meetings. It is a military programme which has changed little in fifty years apart from the study and operation of present day weapons systems. According to Snow, fighters were also encouraged to study military tactics on model battle areas made of clay.

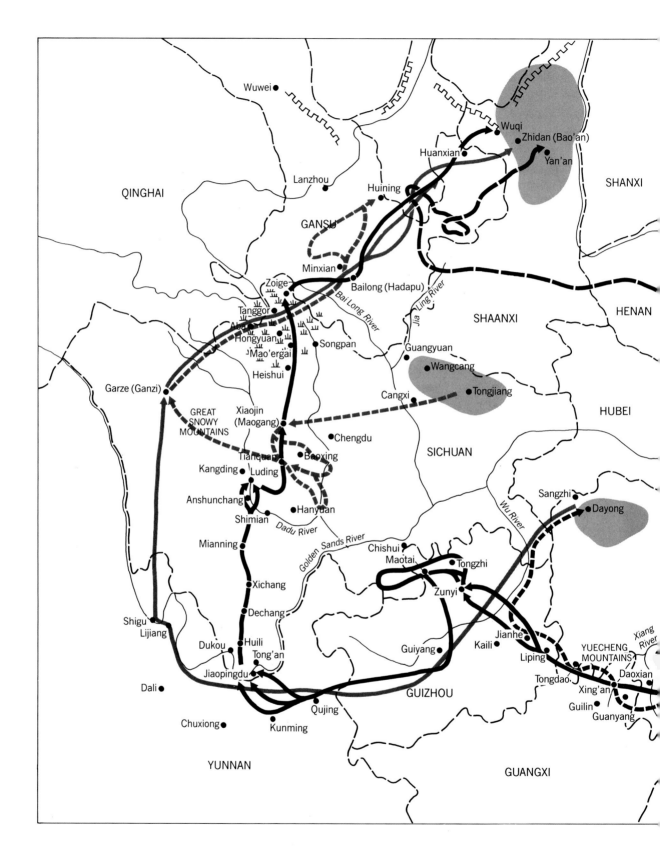

Wuwei

QINGHAI

Lanzhou

Wuqi
Zhidan (Bao'an)
Huanxian
Yan'an

SHANXI

Huining

GANSU

Minxian

Zoige
Bailong (Hadapu)
Tanggor
Aba
Hongyuan
Mao'ergai
Songpan
Heishui

Bai Long River
Jia Ling River

SHAANXI

HENAN

Guangyuan
Wangcang
Tongjiang

Garze (Ganzi)
Cangxi

HUBEI

GREAT
SNOWY
MOUNTAINS

Xiaojin
(Maogang)

Chengdu

SICHUAN

Tianquan
Baoxing
Kangding
Luding

Sangzhi
Dayong

Anshunchang
Shimian
Hanyuan

Dadu River

Mianning

Chishui
Maotai
Tongzhi

Golden Sands River
Wu River

Xichang

Zunyi
Jianhe

Dechang

Shigu
Lijiang

Dukou
Huili
Tong'an
Jiaopingdu

Guiyang
Kaili
Liping

YUECHENG
MOUNTAINS

Xiang River

Daoxian
Tongdao
Xing'an

Dali

GUIZHOU

Qujing
Guilin
Guanyang

Chuxiong
Kunming

YUNNAN

GUANGXI

46

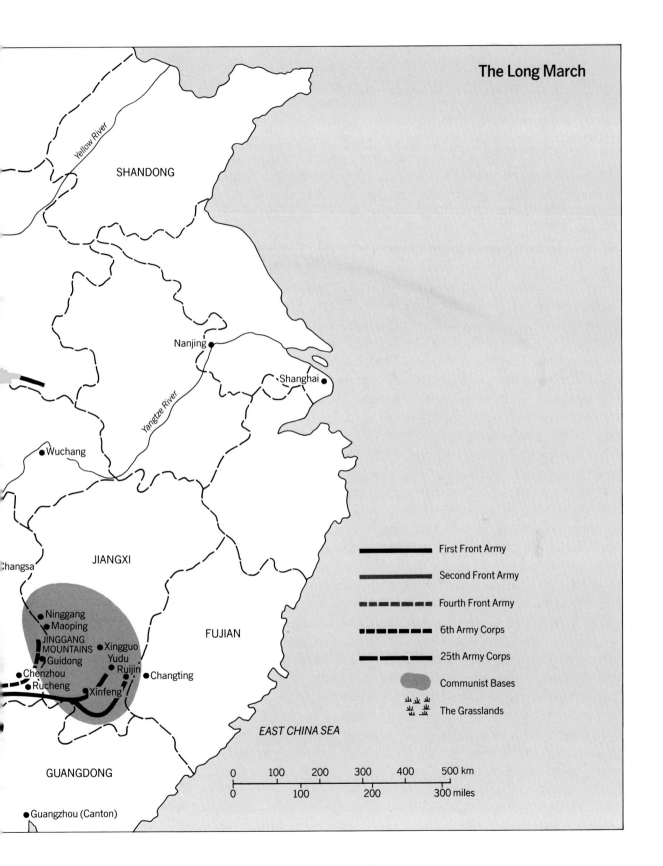

The Long March

SHANDONG

Yellow River

Nanjing

Shanghai

Yangtze River

Wuchang

JIANGXI

Changsa

Ninggang
Maoping
JINGGANG
MOUNTAINS Xingguo
Guidong Yudu
Chenzhou Ruijin
Rucheng Xinfeng Changting

FUJIAN

	First Front Army
	Second Front Army
	Fourth Front Army
	6th Army Corps
	25th Army Corps
	Communist Bases
	The Grasslands

EAST CHINA SEA

GUANGDONG

| 0 | 100 | 200 | 300 | 400 | 500 km |

| 0 | 100 | 200 | 300 miles |

Guangzhou (Canton)

Education also played an important role in the soldier's life. There were writing classes, each soldier being classified by the number of Chinese characters he could write. Each company had some form of simple library, mainly comprised of party political works, supplemented with magazines and newspapers. Opium smoking was non-existent. In fact then, the Red guerrilla fighter was far from being the bacchanalian warrior many Western journalists made him out to be. As Mao pointed out, the army must be one with the people so they realize that it is their army: 'the people are the sea and we are the fish who swim in it.'

Within weeks of setting out in search of their Communist home-land, the Red Army was nearly eradicated at the Battle of Xiang River, in an area just to the north of Guilin in Guangxi Province. Heavily-armed units of the KMT were waiting for the unwieldy fifty-mile column of peasant revolutionaries and their porters as they were about to cross the river. So confident were the Nationalists that they finally could destroy the Communists that their air force showered them with leaflets informing them of their impending slaughter. The week-long battle of Xiang River was a catastrophe for the Red Army. It suffered devastating losses both in manpower and equipment; only a third of the revolutionary force remained – some thirty-thousand fighters and their porters. Morale became a serious problem among the troops; there was disunity among the leaders, and recriminations were rife.

The bedraggled and battle-torn Red Army made its way to Zunyi, a poverty-stricken area of Northern Guizhou, arriving there within a month of the disastrous battle of Xiang River. In Zunyi, the Communists regrouped under Mao, held a turbulent conference and debated their political and ideological differences. Little did the outside world realize that from this obscure Chinese town would emerge decisions and events which would change a nation's destiny.

At the outset of the Long March, the Red Army had uncertain direction; they retreated like the Israelites from the Nationalist Pharaoh, yet without the charismatic leadership of a Moses. After the heated discussions at Zunyi things changed. Mao Tse-tung, the peasant-lover, and political tactician, emerged as the firm leader of the Communist revolution. Here was the Moses who had overcome the Russian protagonists within the Chinese Communist Party and who would lead his people from the political wilderness to the egalitarian Promised Land.

The Red Army, with Mao's leadership now firmly established and Chu Teh as its military tactician, was once again filled with

In its campaigns against the Communist forces Chiang Kai-shek's Nationalist army had the benefit of large numbers of aircraft which were used with great effect in the pursuit of the enemy.

revolutionary zeal. Politics aside, the rest period at Zunyi had been good for the troops. It had given them time to lick their wounds and reorganize. Everyone, it seems, had been able to replenish his or her personal supplies; each soldier had received a little money, new footwear, good food and fresh medical supplies. Most important of all, commanders now had firm objectives: a Yangtze crossing, which was imperative, then a march north to join their Fourth Army comrades. It would not be easy: Chiang's troops were guarding every possible crossing point of the river. But by now the Red guerrillas were masters of deception, and by a series of simple manoeuvres they outwitted the Nationalist forces and crossed the Golden Sands River – as the Yangtze is known in those parts. Thereafter they made their way north.

Following Zunyi, there is little doubt that Mao sensed it would be to his advantage eventually to join forces with Zhang Guotao's Fourth Front Army in Northern Sichuan. His informants had told him it was an army that was well led and, more importantly, well armed and supplied. Their added fire power would be to his advantage, for he realized that by the time they met, his fighters would be exhausted and in need of supplies.

Zhang Guotao, Commander of the Fourth Front Army, was a

seasoned revolutionary, born into a land-owning family and trained in Moscow. A founder member of the Chinese Communist Party, he was a proud and assiduous leader with more than a touch of belligerence in his nature. He had little regard for Mao and considered the Shaoshan village boy uneducated and uncouth. They shared little political harmony; Zhang favoured the Soviet brand of communism, while Mao was already developing China's own form of socialism. Zhang certainly saw himself as China's future leader and, in his pursuit of leadership, Mao was an obstacle.

The long-awaited reunion of the armies of Mao and Zhang Guotao at Fubian in Southern Shaanxi was a total disaster. No sooner had the joys of meeting subsided than the two leaders were at each other's throats.

Although they agreed to travel northwards, each by his own route, there was every indication that Zhang had treachery in his mind and planned a coup with the intention of overthrowing Mao's forces.

He was always opposed to Mao's idea of establishing a base in Northern Shaanxi, distrusting Mao and instinctively preferring the seclusion of Western Sichuan. He believed there was greater

During the Long March the Red Armies suffered devastating losses from the Nationalist forces, local war-lords and, even more than these, the hardships of the desolate terrain. When all this was finally behind them, the First, Second and Fourth Front Armies joined forces at Huining in Gansu Province. There were days of celebrations and the town was draped in banners and flags. Many of the Long March leaders were there including Lin Biao, Peng Dehuai, Nie Rongzhen, and Zhang Guotao. This photograph shows the first unit of the Fourth Front Red Army in Huining.

security nearer to the Soviet border in Xinjiang and he had been assured of Russian help if he could get there. Finally, after months of acrimony, this rift within the Red Army was healed at the historic meeting in Huining in October 1936.

The darkest hour for the Red Army, during the closing stages of the Long March, was the annihilation of the élite Fourth Front Army, when it made its way westward to establish a Communist enclave under the leadership of Zhang Guotao. Only a handful of this once great army survived. They eventually found their way back to the main Red Army base in Bao'an, which by this time was beginning to flourish under Mao's leadership.

Of all the Fathers of the Revolution, perhaps Zhang Guotao was instinctively the most prudent of all. He defected to the Kuomintang, then fled to Hong Kong, and was last heard of in Canada. During the Cultural Revolution, all Mao's comrades of the Long March suffered: Chou Enlai was pilloried by Red Guards; the valiant general, He Long, was given a lethal dose of glucose; Liu Shaoqi was tortured and died in prison; Chen Yi, then China's Foreign Minister, died following attacks by Red Guards. The list is endless, and Mao raised not a finger to help any one of them.

In their quest for social equality, many battles and hardships had been faced by the Red Army: surging rivers crossed, mountains scaled, desolate wastelands and marshes overcome where with one false step the unwary perished. And all this was done on empty bellies while doing battle at the same time, not only against the pursuing Nationalists but also against regional warlords, who on many occasions underestimated the ruthless dedication and idealism of these peasant fighters. The Red Army fought them all, and won – though less than twenty thousand of their number survived. Thus, what may have started out as a retreat finally became a fighting pilgrimage, an idealistic journey towards the reality of their Communist Republic.

Fifty years on, there may be many who regard the Long March as a delicate blend of fact, myth and legend. This is for the individual to decide. Whatever the conclusion, it is an epic tale – and perhaps even the Chinese themselves may prefer it this way. Certainly, as long ago as March 1927 in Hunan, Mao had written:

> A revolution is not a dinner party, or writing an essay, or painting a picture, or doing embroidery; it cannot be refined, so leisurely and gentle, so temperate, kind, courteous, restrained and magnanimous. A revolution is an insurrection, an act of violence by which one class overthrows another.

4 The Sino-Japanese War

Understandably, when Mao and his revolutionaries finally arrived in Northern Shaanxi, they did so with a feeling of contentment and euphoria. Here Mao would have time to consider seriously the policies and structure of a future Communist China. Despite being pursued relentlessly for more than a year by overwhelming forces, bombed and shelled without mercy, exposed to perilous terrain and murderous tribesmen, he and his followers had survived, and they had found sanctuary in an almost impregnable area, the desolate hills and valleys around Yan'an.

Although Communist guerrilla forces had been operating within Shaanxi for several years, the arrival of the main body of the Red Army would enable the Communists conclusively to liberate and enlist the peasantry. Now, once and for all, the feudalistic practices of the local landowners would be eradicated. Manchuria, meanwhile, had been invaded by Japan in September 1931 and later became known as Manchukuo. The Japanese consolidated their hold on the territory, and created a 'Peacock Throne' for the last of the Manchu Emperors – Puyi. The Communists, for their part, had declared war on Japan and were gathering nationwide support by appealing to the patriotic spirit of the people, and the catchphrase 'Chinese do not fight Chinese' was coined.

Even though Chiang Kai-shek's supply routes for his armies were stretched and vulnerable, he was obsessed with liquidating the Communists, at the expense of any campaign against the Japanese occupation. His policies were proclaimed with the maxim, 'Pacification first, resistance afterwards'.

Japanese expansionist policies thus continued, mostly unchecked, especially in Northern China. Not even the bombing of Shanghai in 1932, and the massacres by the Japanese which followed, distracted Chiang Kai-shek from his course of action against the Communists. In consequence, Chiang now came under threat even from those who had supported him over many years. The fact that Mao Tse-tung's peasant army had survived all Chiang's attacks and was gaining support in Northern Shaanxi, was enough to intensify criticism from those around him. Every shade of political opinion in China agreed that the fight should be against Japan, and not brother against brother.

Over the previous fifty years Japan had been almost continuously involved in some form of military incursion within China. Adapting to the changing world during the latter part of the nineteenth century, the Japanese Samurai traditionalists had absorbed the best of Western militarism and, seeking to exercise their new-found powers, had fallen upon China. Following a conflict against China in Korea, Japan procured Taiwan. Again, during the Boxer Rebellion, Japan, along with other Treaty Powers, obtained further privileges. Later she fought the Russians, securing the southern half of Manchuria, and ejected them, making the area Japanese sovereign territory. Then, in 1937, Japan made an all-out invasion of China and in the succeeding years occupied large areas of the country – from the Russian border in Northern Manchuria, the whole of Korea (then as far west as Shaanxi Province, near to China's Great Wall) and to the South, beyond the Burmese border. It was to be an eight-year-long occupation, involving three armies in continuous slaughter: the peasant Communist Eighth Route Army, the Nationalist Kuomintang, and the Imperial Japanese Army. It was a bitter struggle, which not only involved high military casualties but also brought tragedy to the civilian population. Japan would not leave Chinese territory until she surrendered to the Allies in 1945.

One of the most bizarre twists of fate involving Chiang Kai-shek occurred at Xian near the ancient site of Chang'an towards the end of 1936. The Generalissimo, as he was often called by the Western press of the time, was threatened by a coup d'état of his own generals and was saved from possible execution by none other than his Communist adversary, Chou Enlai! Continuing his purge against the Communists, Chiang was about to engage in yet another extermination campaign. This time it was to be the newly-established Communist stronghold in the Northern Shaanxi area. By now, with the Imperial Japanese Army about to take Peking, Chiang's commanders saw little purpose in killing their own people, and planned to overthrow him.

This plotting came to the notice of the perceptive Chou Enlai, who intuitively saw danger in Chiang's demise. There was a strong possibility of him being succeeded by a weaker leadership, which could ultimately leave China defenceless against its Japanese invaders. Accordingly, Chou warned Chiang, and joined in the diplomatic persuasions of both Chiang's family and his generals to

bring about an alliance between the armies of the Kuomintang and the Communists. Together, they would fight the common enemy, Japan.

The 'Xian Incident', as it was later to be known, was a major turning point in the fortunes of the Red Army, which would in future be known as the Eighth Front Army. This was not to be an integration of the two political ideologies. The Nationalists and the Communists retained their separate identity and leadership, but it was now no longer illegal to be a Communist and, for the time being at least, the Civil War had ended.

The alliance, although a pragmatic move which postponed the ultimate aim of a Chinese Communist State, was a step which Mao and his comrades had calculated would give them breathing space in which to revitalize their forces and at the same time expose the KMT to the full ferocity of the Japanese. The Northern Shaanxi Communists, who had by now established Yan'an as their base, intuitively knew that one day they would appear as the

The savagery of war: on August 28 1937 Japanese bombers attacked Shanghai railway station, killing two hundred people and leaving countless wounded.

only representatives of China; Mao and his peasant Communist followers moved into their new capital, Yan'an. Mao already saw himself as the Communist Messiah, ready to release China from the injustice of Chiang Kai-shek and his Nationalist administration.

As the Imperial Japanese Army fanned out across Eastern and Northern China, Chiang Kai-shek was forced to move his administrative headquarters further west to Chungking, situated along the upper reaches of the Yangtze, in the province of Sichuan; a safe retreat from the thrust of the Japanese.

Until the outbreak of the Second World War, Nazi Germany had supplied sixty per cent of the Nationalists' arms requirements, in addition to military advisers. Inside China, furthermore, although the KMT still commanded the cities and urban areas, the countryside was controlled by the Communists, where their influence and numbers were increasing.

Nevertheless, Chiang Kai-shek had by now established an international following, and was generally recognized as China's leader. Mao had little recognition from the West; what outside help he received came by way of the USSR.

Although an alliance had been agreed between the Communists and the KMT, there was little honour in their so-called united front. Knowing that ultimately they would encounter each other in a full-scale war, neither side was willing to commit itself to an all-out campaign against the Japanese. Throughout the Japanese occupation of China, neither the Communist nor the Nationalist armies provided any substantial resistance to the might of the Imperial Japanese Army.

After inflicting devastation on the cities, and heavy casualties on the Nationalist Army, the Japanese expected Chiang Kai-shek to negotiate for peace. They planned to make China part of the Japanese Imperial Empire, and then jointly destroy Mao's Communists. But the stubborn Chiang would have none of it, knowing that, sooner or later, the Americans would come to his aid. Indeed, with the escalation of the war in Europe, Chiang Kai-shek realized that it was only a question of time before the Japanese threat was countered by American involvement.

On the morning of December 7 1941 a Japanese naval strike force of six carriers with a total of 450 aircraft commanded by Vice-Admiral Nagumo blasted the American Pacific Fleet at Pearl Harbour, Hawaii. The United States of America was at war.

Meanwhile, Chiang Kai-shek's regime languished in its Yangtze backwater, waiting patiently for the American war machine to sweep through the Pacific islands and come to its aid.

Today, China's militia, which also incorporates People's Armed Departments (PADs), exceeds twelve million. This is Sun Yu-min, a young militia heroine. Following the founding of the People's Republic of China, she attended the National Congress of combat heroes. She is still living and is in good health.

Repeated overtures were made to the Generalissimo by the Allies, asking him to go on the offensive against the Japanese. Chiang, together with his elegant American-educated wife, ignored them all, preferring to save his forces, though they were all corrupt and inefficient, for the moment when he could overthrow the Communists.

There was, however, a growing belief in the international community, which was becoming disenchanted by Chiang's indolence and obsession with eliminating the Communists, that Mao Tse-tung and his Communist fighters offered better hopes for a stable and unified post-War China.

Unlike the lackadaisical Nationalist army in Western China,

56

Mao's Red partisans had increased their hold on the countryside and infiltrated behind the Japanese positions. They became bolder and began operations near the large cities of Peking and Shanghai. With particular effectiveness, they established strong contacts in the provinces of Shandong, Anhui and Henan, gaining vital supplies of food and information from the villagers. Here was ideal country for the Reds to operate in, where each village was a potential partisan stronghold and the presence of inquisitive Japanese patrols would be signalled in advance by friendly villagers. It was the success of the peasants' participation in guerrilla activities that forced the Japanese to take sharp and decisive punitive action against China's urban and peasant population. Knowing the futility of chasing the Reds in alien territory, the Japanese attacked the source of their information and supplies – the peasant villagers – in a campaign of search, burn and destroy.

As the Japanese forces went from village to village, the great suffering they caused had the desired effect of temporarily restricting guerrilla activities. But whatever reservations the peasants might previously have had regarding the ideals and motives of the Communists were now fast disappearing. The Japanese extermination campaign turned thousands into recruits for Mao Tse-tung's revolutionary cause. Thus the Japanese, first by bringing about a united front between the Kuomintang and Communists, no matter how fragile, second by driving the peasants into the Red camp, were unwittingly prime movers in the approaching foundation of the Chinese Communist State.

America too, always reluctant to encourage any form of 'liberal' foreign power, contributed to the Communists' rise by failing to give them official recognition; a policy it was to regret for many years during Mao's leadership. US arms shipments and all the other trappings that an army needs for war, flown in over the Hump by the Americans and an assortment of Allied flyers, were intended solely for the Nationalist war effort, however many of them found their way into Communist hands by the most roundabout routes.

In his campaign to become China's supreme ruler, Chiang Kai-shek was ever anxious to whittle down his Communist adversaries. A typical piece of skulduggery, and one which contributed to the final breakdown in the Communist/Kuomintang alliance, came when Chiang's troops ambushed the rear detachment of the newly-formed Fourth Army as they made their way from their base, south of the Yangtze River, to positions behind the Japanese lines.

Chiang Kai-shek, it must be remembered, was at this time

supreme commander of all Chinese forces. Trapped between the Japanese and the Kuomintang, the Communist unit, reported to have been a non-combat detachment, was totally destroyed and its commander, General Yeh T'ing, taken prisoner. However, Chiang's treachery was not completely successful. The Fourth Army's main force had already crossed the river; the Nationalist trap had been closed too late. Furious at his failure to eliminate his 'Communist allies', Chiang cut off the supplies to any remaining Communist units he could find. He aimed to starve them of money, food and arms. Despite his desperate measures, the Communists continued to harass the Japanese and at the same time confuse Chiang's forces. Inevitably Communist enrolment increased, and their influence intensified and expanded.

It is probable that Chiang Kai-shek had further disloyalty in mind. The Nationalist government in Chungking had the benefit of a never-ending stream of military and political advisers, mainly from the United States. One of them, General Joseph Stillwell, despairing of the apathy and corruption of Chiang's regime and, especially of his preference for eliminating 'Reds' before 'Japs',

The destruction of the enemy's supply lines was one of many harassing tactics which the Red Army and peasant militia groups practised during the Sino-Japanese War.

unearthed convincing evidence that Chiang Kai-shek was prepared to abandon his British and American allies, and was secretly negotiating with the Japanese for them to cease operations against him and thus enable him, once and for all, to wipe out the Communist threat. If the Allies won the war, Chiang saw himself being in a vulnerable position to the Russians, who would come to the aid of the Communists, and in this he saw disaster. But his talks with the Japanese came to nothing. In the meantime the atomic bomb was dropped on Hiroshima, and the world changed.

During the time that the Red Army was operating behind the Japanese lines, they naturally took every opportunity to proselytize the local peasant population on the merits of their cause. Every Red fighter was ordered to be community-orientated, and to become involved in civic work. It is well documented that they helped villages with their harvest, as soldiers in the People's Liberation Army do to this day.

As the Communist armies of Liu Bocheng and He Long infiltrated eastwards, bringing more of the countryside under their influence in the provinces of Hebei and Shandong, Red guerrilla bands also increased their operations and political indoctrination in Southern China. Yan'an, in Northern Shaanxi, was now the Communist homeland, the Mecca of Revolution, and the cradle of the new Communist state. Access to the Red-dominated areas had improved following the formation of the United Front with the Kuomintang. Thousands of political idealists and party supporters made their way from the Japanese-occupied areas to Mao's so-called socialist utopia. Free education was one of the overriding priorities of the new regime; under the presidency of Lin Biao a university was established at Bao'an where two thousand students were admitted. Others studied at various technical institutes. Frugality was a part of their everyday life. Supplies of medicines and arms too were limited. An embarrassed Chiang Kai-shek had to admit that the guerrillas obtained most of their weapons, via the Japanese, from his defeated troops! Weapons captured from the enemy were a mixture of German, British, American and Czechoslovakian rifles and machine-guns. The Mauser machine-pistol was a highly-prized weapon amongst the Red fighters.

Throughout the countryside, where the Communists were in control, significant changes took place. Autocratic landlords lost land to their former peasant workers and taxes were lightened. Opium, prostitution, footbinding, polygamy, arranged marriages, the buying and selling of wives – all practices of China's dynastic past – were eliminated.

Despite all these problems, Mao Tse-tung always looked upon the decade at Yan'an as a honeymoon period. He was able to write military and political papers, chat with his comrades of the March, Chou Enlai, Lin Biao and Chu Teh, and study the works of the social reformers, Marx and Lenin, late into the night. He even found time to play mah-jong with some of the young fighters. It was also a time of marriage problems. Mao had a weakness for a pretty face and He Zizhen, Mao's second wife (his first, Yang Kaihui, having been executed by the KMT in Changsha for refusing to inform on him) was becoming distressed by the presence in Yan'an of the Shanghai actress, Jiang Qing. There is little doubt that she was an opportunist who saw herself sharing the imperial Communist throne with Mao. Besotted by Jiang, he married her, she became a clerk in his office, and in time bore him a daughter. He Zizhen left the mountain stronghold, never to return to Yan'an and quietly drifted into obscurity.

The years in Yan'an were for Mao a time of preparation for his New Society. It was also a time of personal transformation, from being the leader of a nondescript band of peasant rebels to becoming Dictator and Communist Overlord of the vast New China.

'Everyone a soldier' was one of the many slogans of the Chinese revolution, a maxim which is still representative of China's military policy today. Like the ones here, being lectured by their leader, the peasant revolutionary was taught his skills in his village and surrounding countryside.

5 Maoism and the People's Liberation Army

Following the Japanese surrender in 1945 and the withdrawal of their troops, a momentary power vacuum was created in China. But as he made his way to Peking from his Yan'an mountain kingdom, Mao Tse-tung knew exactly what he wanted. For years he had dreamt of nothing else: a Chinese Communist state with himself at its head. Nothing short of total political control, with a government dedicated to Marxist-Leninist ideals, would satisfy him. His Yan'an years had been spent in writing, and in planning his domestic policies.

The Americans however, who together with the other Western Allies had supported Chiang Kai-shek over the years, thought differently. On the day following the cessation of hostilities with Japan, General MacArthur, the Supreme Allied Commander in the Pacific, recognized Chiang Kai-shek as the overall commander of China's military and, as such, authorized him to accept surrenders from isolated pockets of Japanese resistance. China was thrust once again into vicious civil war.

Frantically the Americans now delegated General George C. Marshall to negotiate a ceasefire between the Communists and the Nationalists. Truce talks occurred, and some historians suggest a coalition was mooted. But Mao had little reason to trust the Americans, and was determined to share power with nobody.

Meanwhile, aided by the Americans, Kuomintang troops raced to secure key military positions and secure China's main cities. With the help of the United States Marines, Chiang Kai-shek's troops had early successes in securing roads and railheads leading to Tianjin and Peking. At the same time 100,000 Communist troops commanded by Lin Biao moved into the Manchurian countryside from their bases in Shandong.

At the outset of China's second civil war, also known as the War of Liberation, the over-confident Chiang Kai-shek felt that, with his American support, he would have little trouble in overcoming these peasant renegades, who by now were known as the People's Liberation Army (PLA). But superiority of weapons

and numbers is not in itself a recipe for success in any military campaign; there must also be the will to win and overcome the enemy. Chiang was to be denied the victory which he maintained was his birthright. At this time his Nationalist Force, estimated at three million, outnumbered the PLA by three to one. Chiang Kai-shek's defeat began in Manchuria. Lin Biao's forces systematically picked off the Nationalist-held towns one by one; first surrounding them, then moving in, at which point the Kuomintang usually surrendered.

Thousands of Nationalist troops were now deserting to the Communist armies, with their much-needed supplies and weapons. By the early part of 1948 the Communists had virtually secured Manchuria, which was soon to become the first all-Communist province. In Central China the KMT were faring no better, and in several areas they were completely out-manoeuvred. By April 1948, Jinan, the capital of Shandong, together with the neighbouring province of Henan, were Communist territory.

Chiang Kai-shek made his final desperate stand against the Communists at Suzhou in Northern Anhui. It was a ferocious battle, but even with air support, the Nationalist army failed to hold this vital gateway to the South. Meanwhile at Tianjin the

Sino-Soviet relations have always been fragile: the two countries share a common border of some five thousand miles, a border that is one of the most heavily-defended in the world. This historic moment seems unlikely ever to be repeated; it is the occasion of the citizens of Dalian on the Liaodong Peninsula welcoming Russian troops during their occupation of the area in 1945.

Communist troops halt for a meal during their campaign against the Nationalists in Northern Manchuria, the first area to be completely controlled by the Chinese Red Army. Following the Japanese surrender in 1945 the Communist forces began building up their forces and military equipment: the Soviet Army supplied the PLA with 1,200 cannons and more than 360 tanks as well as 300,000 rifles, 4,800 machine guns and several hundred trucks. By 1949 it was estimated that Communist troops numbered 1,900,000.

battle for the North was taking place and Communist forces were now within a hundred kilometres of Peking and Kuomintang resistance was crumbling. China's capital city fell to the Red Army in January 1949, following a six week long siege. In the weeks that followed there was a brief and unsuccessful attempt at a negotiated surrender by the provisional President, Li Tsung-jen, on behalf of the Nationalists. Communist forces in the South were now in hot pursuit of an enemy that was in total disarray and lacked the will to fight. General Chen Yi's East China Liberation Army, shortly to become the Third Field Army PLA, crossed the Yangtze River in April 1949 on its way to liberate Shanghai and Nanking.

All Nationalist resistance had now collapsed. With his back to the sea, together with the dispirited remnants of his army, Chiang Kai-shek fled to the island of Formosa, now known as Taiwan, leaving behind him a desolate country, war-torn and bankrupt, its industry ruined. The man whom the West had thought of as

China's saviour died in Taiwan in relative obscurity in 1975.

Mao Tse-tung, on October 1 1949, standing where China's emperors had stood before, looked out across a sea of cheering faces in Peking's Tiananmen Square and announced the formation of the People's Republic of China. Commentators at the time sardonically referred to Mao as China's first 'Red Emperor', but he barely noticed his critics. After years in the wilderness and overcoming his enemies both inside and outside the Party, he was finally China's supreme ruler.

With the establishment of the People's Republic of China (PRC) and following the War of Liberation, the PLA, as China's national army, not only under-pinned Mao's new regime, being responsible for the internal and external defence of the country, but also in certain areas became involved in the administration of civil government. As in their Red Army days, the PLA not only provided for themselves, but also set to work with the people: industry was rebuilt, roads and railways repaired and, in the countryside, crops were planted and harvested.

No sooner had the PLA begun to recover from defeating the

Celebrations in Datong, Shanxi Province on May 1 1949 after KMT forces had surrendered to the PLA.

The People's Republic of China finally became a reality on October 1 1949. Thousands gathered in Tiananmen Square to hear Mao Tse-tung's declaration of the new Republic; beside him was Liu Shaoqi who was to become Head of State and second only to Mao within the Party.

Nationalists in the War of Liberation than Mao involved them in further confrontations: the invasion of Tibet and the Korean War. With only the faintest murmurings, the world stood by in the summer of 1950 and witnessed seven divisions of the PLA invade Tibet, bringing the area under Communist domination. Korea, however, was a different matter.

When a force of some 300,000 Chinese troops of the Fourth Field Army crossed the Yalu River into North Korea in October 1950 in support of their comrades in North Korea, they did not do so as China's national army, the PLA. To minimize world criticism, and to avoid the possibility of creating a state of war between China and the United States, the Chinese designated the invading force a 'volunteer' one. So it was that the PLA contingents who fought in the Korean War were always referred to as the Chinese People's Volunteers (CPVs).

The Volunteers were commanded by a veteran fighter of the Long March, forty-eight year old Peng Dehuai, later to be appointed a Marshal in the PLA and Minister of Defence. All his life Peng had

been a soldier and guerrilla fighter. At twenty-eight he had been a brigade commander with the Kuomintang. Later, joining the Communists, along with Lin Biao he led the vanguard from Southern Jiangxi at the outset of the Long March.

The Korean War, however, was a salutary experience for the PLA; for the first time they were in combat against a modern adversary, an international force capable of delivering intensive firepower, both from the air and on the ground.

During the early weeks of the campaign, despite their deficiencies in weaponry and communications, the first attacks were successful; but the United Nations force overcame this form of attack by developing greater flexibility along their established fronts.

Fearing a Communist defeat, the Russians came to the aid of the Chinese, supplying them with military equipment which included aircraft and much-needed pilot training. Had Soviet aid not been available, the eventual stalemate in this conflict could well have been avoided. Russia's intervention was a powerful catalyst in the subsequent modernization of the PLA.

Speaking to me about the Korean Campaign at his Oxfordshire home, General Sir Anthony Farrar-Hockley, Adjutant of the First Battalion of the Gloucester Regiment during the Korean War, who was captured by the North Koreans, imprisoned by the Chinese and subsequently interrogated and tortured following the battle of Imjin River in April 1951, says of the conflict:

> The Korean War changed the whole basis of the PLA, in as much as
> it went into Korea as Mao's obedient tool – root and branch – and it

While every effort is being made to modernize the PLA and to improve its mobility, the old well-tried methods of transport are retained in some areas, notably the Gobi Desert. Here the Bactrian camel is preferred; its build and thick coat make it the best form of transport for mountain and desert. On these camel patrols the PLA are assisted by the People's Militia who have an intimate knowledge of the local areas.

came out some three years later disenchanted with his leadership. This was because they had been told that weapons were not the first matter of importance, but men, and above all, men's spirit and attitude. They had lost hundreds of thousands of men because they lacked the right equipment and weapons. They had also lost the best of the political officers who had either been killed or severely wounded in battle. The result was that they never again trusted Mao or were his absolutely reliable servants.

There was a rising movement in the services that was quick to see that there had to be change once Mao had gone and the era of the little Red Book was over. So Chou Enlai was secretly in favour of improvements to weaponry in all the main services and when Deng Xiaoping came to power he was of the same opinion.

When hostilities ceased in Korea in 1953 the PLA's leaders, in particular its commander there, Peng Dehuai, were well aware that it would take some considerable time for the army to recover. One thing was certain as far as Peng was concerned: China must modernize its military forces with the minimum of delay. Peng Dehuai was revered by the PLA and as Acting Chairman of the Party's Military Affairs Commission (MAC) which embodied the office of Minister of Defence and Joint Chiefs of Staff, he was highly respected by the Politburo of which he was a member.

Mao Tse-tung obviously envied the popularity which Peng received both from the military and the Politburo and wrongly believed this veteran military commander was a threat to his own leadership. In fact one of Mao's female fighters has said that he was an insecure man, whose dislike of intellectuals and the arts was based on his own inability to understand them. It was even rumoured, she said, that most of his poetry was written for him. It would appear that many of her comrades had much greater admiration for Peng Dehuai, whom they adored. But no one, other than Mao, ever questioned Peng's loyalty. Mao's growing suspicions were further aroused when Peng challenged him during a Party conference in 1959 on the question of the PLA's future policies, and China's increasingly fragile relationship with the Soviet Union. In Peng's reasoning, sound Soviet relationships were essential to the success of the PLA's modernization programme. Mao disagreed, and in consequence the veteran guerrilla fighter, who had fought the Nationalists, Japanese and the Americans, one of the PLA's most distinguished leaders, was summarily dismissed from office and replaced by Lin Biao. Many people, certainly the military, regarded Peng's unjustifiable sacking as one of Mao's greatest errors. Peng's death in 1974 was not revealed to the Chinese people until six years later.

While the PLA was busy involving itself with its own

modernization programme, another revolution was quietly simmering within the Communist Party's political machine. The Great Proletarian Cultural Revolution burst upon the nation in the early 1960s with a savagery comparable to any of the civil wars' atrocities. To what extent this national purge was brought about by Mao alone is difficult to assess. In its viciousness it could well be partly attributed to his wife Jiang Qing, who was by now a powerful manipulator of China's politics, and greatly feared by Mao's associates.

For Mao, the 'Great Leap Forward' of 1958 had been a disaster and by the early 1960s, with his power base weakening, he clearly felt it was time to reinforce his autocratic leadership within the Party, and rid himself of many of his political adversaries and critics. In a skilful move Mao and the tight band of political supporters which surrounded him carried out their purification campaign by directing the masses of the peasants and workers to return to the true spirit of revolution. Hundreds of thousands of government personnel, educators, writers, artists, doctors, film makers and industrial workers were 'transported' to the agricultural communes to begin a rectification programme. Few people, especially those connected with the arts, escaped the purge; even Chou Enlai only narrowly escaped being beaten by Red Guards. And it was Lin Biao, Mao's Defence Minister and heir apparent, supported by the PLA, who gave Mao the power to implement his political reforms and conduct his witch hunts. Paradoxically, evidence indicates that Lin, faithful servant of Mao, had plans to assassinate his leader and take over the country aided no doubt by the PLA. Whatever the plans, they went wrong. Anticipating his demise in 1971, Lin sought sanctuary in the Soviet Union but never arrived. Some reports say that the plane was shot down by pursuing fighters; it is unlikely that the outside world will ever know the truth of these statements.

The consequences of the Cultural Revolution were felt in every city, village and hamlet throughout China. The toll of human suffering was horrific. 400,000 Chinese are reported to have died by violence, five hundred party leaders were imprisoned, more than thirty are known to have been tortured to death, twenty were maimed and sixty driven insane. It was not until the death of Mao in 1976 that the country regained its national self-esteem.

Whether the PLA was involved in the chicanery and politics of the Cultural Revolution by accident or design is difficult to say. However, it is undeniable that without PLA intervention China could have been plunged into total anarchy, leading almost

Detachments of the PLA entering Lhasa. Following Indian independence, eastern parts of Tibet came under Chinese sovereignty. The PLA occupied Tibet in 1949; ten years later there was a Tibetan revolt and the PLA moved into the area in force. By way of explanation to the West, the Chinese government claimed to be 'liberating' the Tibetans from subversive elements within the country. Tibetans still regard themselves as being occupied by the Chinese, however, while the Chinese maintain that there is a peaceful and understanding co-existence between the two peoples. The Chinese government is extremely sensitive about the control of Tibet and all foreign visitors are strictly supervised.

certainly to a third civil war.

Since Korea, China has been involved in two serious border disputes: one with India, the other with Vietnam. Along China's five-thousand-mile northern border with the Soviet Union there have been the occasional 'firefights' which, following the usual diplomatic protests, have ceased within a few days. Serious open warfare, however, broke out between China and India in October 1962 concerning a border dispute. During the conflict PLA forces advanced approximately a hundred miles into Indian territory along two fronts; Kashmir and an area east of Bhutan, before withdrawing. From that time, along with other Asian countries, India has regarded China as a country with expansionist aspirations. In recent years there have been a series of border clashes along China's southern border with Vietnam, some more serious than others. On the pretext of coming to the aid of Kampuchea and following the signing of a Vietnamese-Russian Treaty, the PLA invaded Vietnam during the early part of 1979. Much to their surprise, having underestimated the capabilities of Vietnamese forces, the PLA sustained heavy losses: 26,000 killed and 37,000 wounded. Realizing then that they could be drawn into a long and protracted confrontation, the Chinese withdrew, but conscious of their damaged prestige engaged in probing actions across their southern border. These have resulted ever since in virtually continuous hostilities between China and Vietnam.

Perhaps more than anything else since Mao's death the restructuring and modernization of the PLA, coupled with its re-education, is one of the most significant reforms in the development of China. Much to the delight of the Chinese, military improvements have been accomplished without any apparent excessive increase in defence spending or drain upon the country's precious foreign exchange reserves. In recent years, China's innovative arms industry has greatly improved its overseas sales to the Middle East, principally brought about by the Iran-Iraq war which broke out in 1980. Arms sales to Iran, including Silkworm missiles worth £250 million, is believed to total well in excess of one billion pounds. China is also believed to have supplied Iraq with fighters, F6s and F7s, Type 69 battle tanks, artillery and various automatic weapons.

Crucial to any understanding of the PLA is the awareness that they have a powerful influence within Chinese society. The world has been all too ready to accept at face value the often-quoted Maoist dictum: 'the Party commands the gun, and the gun must never be allowed to command the Party.' The reality is that military and political life in China are enmeshed in a tight embrace. Mao and his followers have always known, as do China's current leaders, that it is the gun which commands the Party and that the PLA is likely to remain the most revolutionary organization in China.

China has always been a secret and conspiratorial society and as the reign of Deng Xiaoping, the great survivor of Chinese politics, draws to a close, there are signs that a new revolution is brewing. As his successors scramble for power in the political corridors of Peking, without warning the 'open door' proffered to the West is beginning to close and observers in China are speaking of an icy wind of change which is blowing around Tiananmen Square.

The People's Liberation Army for some time now has maintained a relatively low profile, lurking in Peking's authoritarian shadows, cautiously observing the shifting political sands. In the event of any political upheaval, it is the only force that will be capable of maintaining national unity.

PART 2
CHINA 1986

1 China Tea in Swiss Cottage

January 1985, London

From as far back as I can remember, I have always wanted to go to China. The road there in my case was by way of Swiss Cottage, that area of London lying to the north of Baker Street in the capital's Borough of Camden. Although clearly an unusual route, this turned out to be an excellent way to the former land of the Khans – now the home of cadres and commissars in the world's most populous Communist state.

The January morning was damp and soggy. I recall that it was the second week of the month – round about the tenth – when I made my way down Eton Avenue in NW3 for my meeting with the Military Attaché of the People's Republic of China.

As I hurried past the rows of elegant red-bricked Victorian houses, bare hawthorn trees splayed against their white bay windows, I wondered how I would be received by the Chinese. All governments are sensitive about their armed forces; and here I was bringing a request to be allowed to photograph, and write about, their military. Naturally I was apprehensive about their reaction.

Partly secluded by evergreens, number ten looked as if it served as both home and office – as many diplomatic residences do. Its ornate architecture was similar to many of the other houses in Eton Avenue built in russet-red brick, with a tiled roof of the same colour and a small turreted tower in the left-hand corner. Nearby, just off Winchester Road, mechanics in a row of dingy garages repaired ageing cars. At one time, the Victorian professional class who lived here had them as their stables. Now the developers and refurbishers had moved in with builders working mechanical diggers and pneumatic drills. Through the noise, Irish dialects mingled with accents from north of the Tweed.

At that time, Mr Feng Zhenyao was the Military Attaché at the Chinese Embassy and it was one of his staff that opened the door. Smiling, and with a gentle sweep of the hand, he motioned me to enter. From the gloomy interior of the Victorian entrance hall, Mr Feng himself stepped forward and shook my hand. 'Welcome, Mr

Young – please.' Walking on, he indicated that I should follow.

Everything about the room I entered reflected China. Only the moulded Victorian ceiling betrayed its nineteenth-century European origins. On the walls hung scroll-like Chinese paintings of horses with flying tails, and mountains shaped like sharks' teeth, with brush strokes that went from coal black tar to a wispy grey. A glass cabinet displayed a collection of ivory and jade carvings. Above all else, however, it was the dainty white embroidered crochet covers on the claret-red sofa and chairs that first caught my eye. Each of the arms and headrests had them. They were to become a familiar sight in every military establishment and hotel I was to visit during my stay in China. 'Please,' said Mr Feng, indicating that I should sit. I chose a corner of one of the large wine-coloured sofas. He sat in the other.

Mr Feng was thin and willowy, and despite his official title certainly lacked the usual physique of most military men. Seated there taking notes, he gave the impression of being more at home in the classroom than the barracks. His face reflected an almost stoic quality. As the sharp morning light from the large bay window cut across the room, it gave his face the appearance of pale yellow jade. But yet, behind the Oriental impassiveness there clearly was a sense of humour and fun. I had little difficulty imagining Mr Feng doing his Taijiquan exercises at sunrise in the courtyard of his home in Peking.

All my discussions with the Chinese, both in Britain and China, began with tea; a civilized custom which we in the West have all but lost to the American habit of tasteless coffee in polystyrene cups. Taking the lids from two elegant, blue, patterned porcelain cups, Mr Feng poured hot water onto the leaves in them from a large thermos jug by the table, replacing their lids to retain the heat in the pale golden liquid.

His English was slow and deliberate and, very much in the British tradition, we talked about London and the weather. Eventually he came to the point. 'I believe you wish to produce a book about China; how can I help? Please, take some tea.'

Removing the lid from the delicate cup I tasted my first cup of China tea in years. The light-coloured liquid was delicious. I had forgotten how refreshing it could be.

'I would like the People's Republic of China to give me permission to produce a book on the People's Liberation Army. Broadly speaking, it will be a picture book with text, an historical document, telling the story of the PLA from its Red Army beginnings to the present day. It would require the total co-operation of all three armed services. I would like to begin as soon as permission is granted.'

Mr Feng watched me intently and took another sip of tea, his face betraying nothing. 'Tell me, what kind of things would you like to see in the PLA?'

I replied, 'Here in the West we know so little about China. I would like to meet as many PLA personnel as your government will allow.' Mentioning my recent book on the French Foreign Legion, I tactfully pointed out the excellent facilities the government of France had made available to me. 'Perhaps, in your letter to the Ministry of Defence, you could request something similar, on my behalf.'

Mr Feng smiled and went on making notes. Mentally, I had rehearsed this many times. My presentation would be quiet yet positive. Under no circumstances must I offend by being too demanding. The lovely oriental expression of bending with the wind lingered at the back of my mind. I recalled a comment by a Chinese general speaking of American troops during the Korean War. 'They do not understand bamboo,' he said.

Finally, making sure he had the right English words, Mr Feng said: 'I think your book will be very good for the friendship of our two countries. Before I write to the Ministry of Defence in Beijing recommending your project, send me a letter explaining everything you require.'

He rose from the sofa, indicating that our meeting was over. As he helped me with my coat, he reminded me to write as soon as possible. 'It may be some time before I receive a reply from Beijing – so don't worry.' He shook my hand and thanked me for coming.

It was now much warmer outside, as a pale January sun filtered through the silver birches along the avenue. At least I could take comfort from the fact that my proposal had not been rejected outright. Now it was for Peking to decide.

Three months later, during the second week of April, Mr Feng telephoned again asking me to come and see him as he had just received a message from Peking.

There was a whiff of spring in the air and a touch of colour was creeping around the branches of the lime and ash trees outside Mr Feng's window. He looked up from what appeared to be rather a long and complicated communication from Peking. 'The Ministry of Defence would like certain things clarified regarding your visit to China. I hope you don't mind my asking some more questions. You do understand – everything has to be referred to our leaders in Beijing.' He was most apologetic. Clearly there was still a degree of uncertainty regarding my visit.

'Beijing has asked me which political party you belong to.' Mr Feng was clearly ill at ease at having to ask the question. 'I have tried to explain that Britain is a conservative country...' He was having difficulty finding the right words. I interrupted without discovering if he meant conservative with a large or small 'c'.

'I am not a political person Mr Feng. For most of my life I have been involved in documenting world events. As a photojournalist I try not to involve myself in politics.'

I suspect that Mr Feng was rather perplexed; being politically neutral must be difficult for a Communist to fathom. He nodded and continued making notes.

One of the more noticeable changes that has come about within the PLA recently is the change of uniform. Gone are the baggy pyjama-styled green uniforms, complete with Jiefang Maozi Liberation Hat and Red Star. Now the Army, the Navy and the Air Force each has its own distinctive dress.

To help to overcome Mr Feng's confusion, I asked him about the new uniforms. 'One moment, I will show you. I received mine a few days ago,' he replied, rushing out of the room to return a few minutes later proudly displaying his new uniform on a coathanger. My first impression was that the olive green uniform with its brass buttons had an Eastern Bloc look about it. The matching hat, with black peak and heavy grey braid, appeared larger than those worn by our own troops. The small plastic red star, of earlier years, was replaced by one in metal, set against a blue background. On the five-pointed star were the Chinese characters depicting the commemorative date of the founding of the Red Army, August 1. The hat was trimmed with a red band and piping.

The shoulder boards on the tunic were almost square. Each had a small metal red star engraved with the August 1 character. A brown leather belt and olive green trousers completed the uniform.

As I examined the hat and tunic it occurred to me that I must be one of the first people in Britain to see the new PLA uniform at close quarters. 'How do you like it Mr Feng, compared to the old one?' I asked.

He did not answer straight away. Instead he looked proudly at the uniform for a few moments, then cautiously replied, 'Yes – I think it is much better.'

We went on to discuss accommodation. From my point of view nothing could be better than being invited to stay in PLA barracks, which would give me the rare opportunity to gain an insight into Chinese military life that few Westerners have experienced, but at the time I thought it unlikely that the Chinese authorities would agree. Mr Feng, however, felt there would be no difficulty. 'Once the Ministry of Defence has approved your visit this sort of thing would depend on the local Commander of the Unit.' He paused before going on to explain that there might be a small charge.

There was more sipping of tea and I then departed, wondering if I was any nearer to China and the PLA.

It is always the same. Things happen when you least expect them. Answering the telephone one morning a few weeks later I was surprised to hear the hesitating voice of Mr Feng. 'Mr Robert Young – I have some good news for you. The MOD has approved your visit to China. When can you come and see me to arrange a date for your departure?'

A week later I met Mr Feng to discuss the details of my trip. The choice of the right season to arrive in China was critical. Peking winter temperatures can drop well below zero and last from November to March. Spring would also have its problems because of the dust storms which blow in from the Gobi desert, sprinkling a yellow powder everywhere and covering the whole area with a fine yellow blanket. The summer months of June and July were finally agreed: it might be unpleasantly hot, well into the eighties, but it seemed that June was the best time for the Ministry of Defence to receive me.

For the next hour Mr Feng and I discussed accommodation and travel arrangements; for although I was to be a guest of the Chinese government, I was paying for everything myself. From my very earliest days as a photojournalist I have made it a rule to accept only limited hospitality. By doing this I maintain my independence and objectivity.

My departure was planned for early June and the all-important visa number 95015 was stamped in my passport, even though the final permission for my journey had not yet arrived from Peking.

A few days before my departure Mr Chen Wen Qing, the new Military Attaché, called me. In a clear, almost Oxbridge accent, he requested details of my flight and told me I would be met on arrival. With a 'Hope you will enjoy your stay in China', he rang off.

It was 9.12 am on June 4 1986 when I checked in at London's Heathrow Terminal Four for flight BA 003 to Peking routing by Rome, Bahrain, and Hong Kong, a journey of twenty hours or more, covering some ten thousand miles.

Flight BA 003 appeared on the monitor screen and I made my way to the departure gate; finally the doors to China and the People's Liberation Army were opening.

2 Peking: Comrades and Cadres

Peking Capital Airport has a sterile atmosphere; although it is said to have been inspired by Paris's Orly Airport, it lacks the sense of style that the French put into most things. Still, the buildings have all the usual modern facilities, even air-conditioning, which is a great benefit to the weary traveller arriving in the heat of the Peking summer.

My first business transaction in Communist China was a clear indication that the new capitalist spirit of free enterprise was flourishing there. It was a matter of the airport trolley: as I attempted to help myself from a line of neatly parked trolleys, the

As China's economy improves, so private and public transport is on the increase. Peking's Fuxingmen Avenue resembles the main roads of many Western cities during the rush hour.

young Chinese girl guarding them held out her hand. There was no doubt about it – payment was expected! For a few coins the trolley complete with her porterage services were mine. My luggage and equipment were piled high onto it. Swaying through the customs with the minimum of formalities, I walked out into the bright summer sunlight followed by my small Chinese porter.

As I was a guest of the Ministry of Defence, I had been assured that someone would meet me. Peering through the crowds around the terminal exit I saw my name written in large block letters on a piece of card held against the chest of one of two men who were peering at the faces of the departing passengers. We saw each other at the same time, and the two men smiled broadly as I approached. They were dressed in casual clothes, open-necked white cotton shirts worn loosely over light-weight trousers. Both wore black leather sandals on stockinged feet.

'My name is Mr Gu Jingshu, your interpreter,' said the smaller of the two, 'and this is Mr Chen Detung, from the PLA Pictorial. We have a car waiting. Please, this way.' He pointed towards a gleaming black Toyota Crown car parked nearby. The driver had

Evening sunlight on the Golden Water Stream enhances the air of mystery and intrigue that has always been associated with the Imperial Palace, commonly referred to as the Forbidden City by Western visitors. Its splendours were hidden from public view until the founding of the Republic of China in 1912. The Imperial Palace covers 250 acres, is three quarters of a mile long and half a mile wide.

The tiles of imperial yellow which cover almost every roof of the Forbidden City had a symbolic meaning during the dynastic period, indicating that the Imperial Palace was the centre of the Earth.

already opened the large boot and was ready to load my baggage.

One of the first things I noticed on the way to Peking city centre were the long avenues of trees on either side of the road, mostly young poplars and willows which had been planted, I was told, as part of the government's tree growing programme which could be seen throughout the neighbouring agricultural communities.

By all accounts the old Peking had been a magnificent sight, its fortifications rising majestically from the surrounding North China Plain. Old photographs show the city after a snowfall; its walls and turrets finely etched against snow and sky, an elegant reminder of China's Imperial past. Vandalized by progress, however, walls, turrets and arches of the former Manchu city were pulled down over thirty years ago. Centuries of history were swept away by the Communist government in the pursuit of progress – mostly to ease

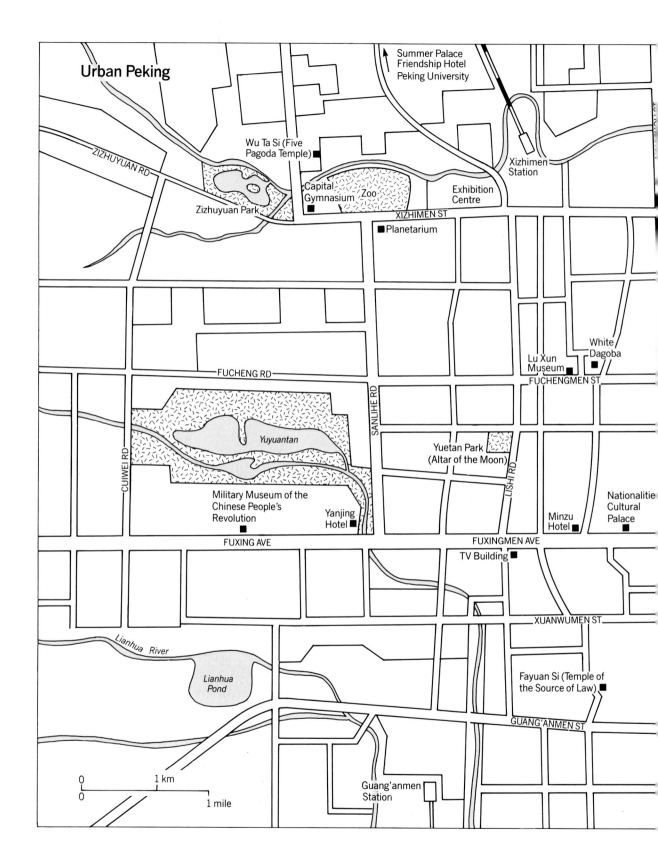

Urban Peking

ZIZHUYUAN RD

Summer Palace
Friendship Hotel
Peking University

Wu Ta Si (Five
Pagoda Temple) ■

Capital
Gymnasium ■

Zoo

Zizhuyuan Park

Xizhimen
Station

Exhibition
Centre

XIZHIMEN ST

■ Planetarium

FUCHENG RD

SANLIHE RD

Yuyuantan

CUIWEI RD

Military Museum of the
Chinese People's
Revolution ■

Yanjing
Hotel ■

FUXING AVE

Lu Xun
Museum ■

White
Dagoba ■

FUCHENGMEN ST

Yuetan Park
(Altar of the Moon)

LISHI RD

Nationalitie
Cultural
Palace ■

Minzu
Hotel ■

FUXINGMEN AVE

TV Building ■

XUANWUMEN ST

Lianhua River

Lianhua
Pond

Fayuan Si (Temple of
the Source of Law) ■

GUANG'ANMEN ST

0   1 km
0
                1 mile

Guang'anmen
Station

80

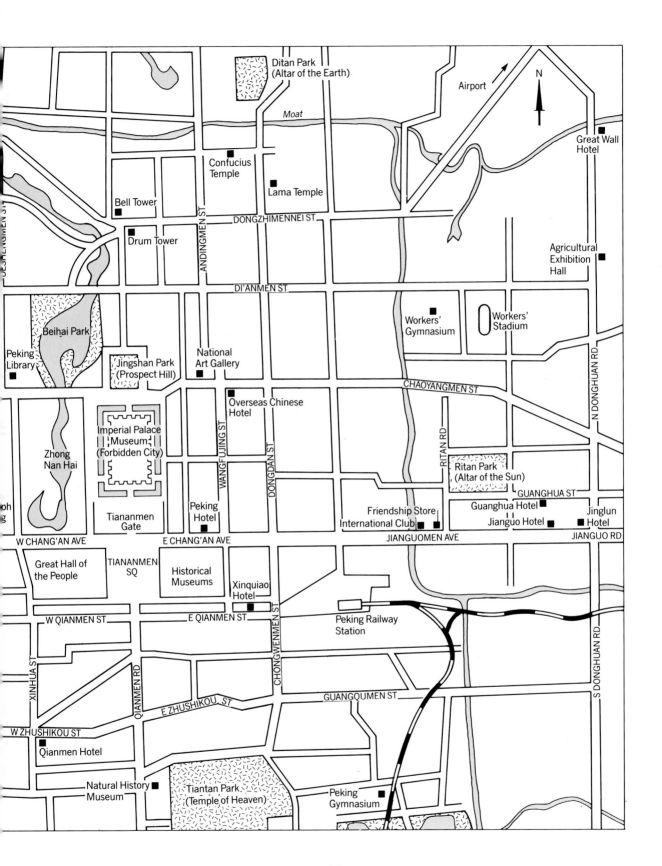

Ditan Park
(Altar of the Earth)

Airport

N

Moat

Great Wall
Hotel

Confucius
Temple

Lama Temple

Agricultural
Exhibition
Hall

Bell Tower

ANDINGMEN ST

DONGZHIMENNEI ST

Drum Tower

DI'ANMEN ST

Beihai Park

Workers'
Gymnasium

Workers'
Stadium

Peking
Library

Jingshan Park
(Prospect Hill)

National
Art Gallery

CHAOYANGMEN ST

N DONGHUAN RD

Overseas Chinese
Hotel

WANGFUJING ST

RITAN RD

Zhong
Nan Hai

Imperial Palace
Museum
(Forbidden City)

DONGDAN ST

Ritan Park
(Altar of the Sun)

GUANGHUA ST

Guanghua Hotel

Guanghua Hotel

oh
g

Tiananmen
Gate

Peking
Hotel

Friendship Store
International Club

Jiango Hotel

Jinglun
Hotel

W CHANG'AN AVE

E CHANG'AN AVE

JIANGUOMEN AVE

JIANGUO RD

Great Hall of
the People

TIANANMEN
SQ

Historical
Museums

Xinquiao
Hotel

CHONGWENMEN ST

S DONGHUAN RD

W QIANMEN ST

E QIANMEN ST

Peking Railway
Station

XINHUA ST

QIANMEN RD

E ZHUSHIKOU ST

GUANGQUMEN ST

W ZHUSHIKOU ST

Qianmen Hotel

Natural History
Museum

Tiantan Park
(Temple of Heaven)

Peking
Gymnasium

the city's traffic problems.

With China now being opened up to travel-hungry Westerners, hotel accommodation in Peking is both scarce and expensive. Unless the visitor is part of a group tour or, like myself, benefiting from the assistance of government cadres, accommodation is difficult to obtain. The capital's hotels are fully booked months in advance. This is becoming an embarrassment to the Chinese tourist industry but hotel construction in all the main tourist areas has so far failed to keep pace with an increasing demand.

A government official admitted to me that foreign investors are nervous of any long-term commitment to China's tourist industry. They demand a return within five years on their capital, and consequently, the cost of hotel accommodation is spiralling upwards. Everyone in China is allotted a *danwei*. Briefly the *danwei* is a work unit which controls and monitors the individual from the cradle to the grave. The *danwei* has been described as the building block of Chinese society. The system can even affect foreigners, who like myself are involved with government officials. At various times during the early days of my visit searching questions were asked concerning my background: Who did I work for? How much did I earn? Was my work well known? No doubt my answers enabled my hosts to place me within a *danwei* so giving some indication at what level I should be received within the PLA.

My hosts had chosen the eleven-storey Min Zu Hotel, conveniently situated in the central part of Peking on the north side of Fuxingmen Avenue. The following afternoon I met the two cadres in my hotel room, as arranged. Sleep and a bath had worked wonders after the exhausting twenty-hour flight from London. Mr Chen arrived carrying a small holdall from which he produced six slender books, with two-tone brown covers, which he told me had just been published. Here was the photographic index covering the history of the People's Revolution and the Red Army, from its beginnings until the founding of the Communist Republic in 1949. Leafing slowly through each volume, I was astounded at what I saw: page after page of vivid black and white images, picturing China's turbulent history. 'You are the first Westerner to see these books,' Mr Chen told me. 'You may keep them until tomorrow to make your selection.' Choosing from so many photographs would not be easy and I knew I was going to have a late night.

There is a definite reticence in all nations when asked to reveal and discuss anything about their military forces, and clearly Chinese officials are still extremely suspicious of foreign journalists, regardless of the so-called new liberalism towards the West. I had hoped to have appointments in government offices, walk through Peking's corridors of power and be allowed to glimpse into the offices of China's Communist mandarins. But this was to be denied me. All discussions and arrangements for my visits to the various PLA units were arranged in my hotel room.

First I was told to write down everything I wanted to photograph and visit within the PLA. Mr Gu warned me to include as much detail as possible, as once approval had been finalized there could be no amendments. Some of my demands were outrageous and I knew it. But over the years I have always approached these situations with the philosophy that if you don't ask, you don't get...

So when I asked, for example, to be taken to troop positions along the Vietnamese border and into the remoter regions of Tibet, I

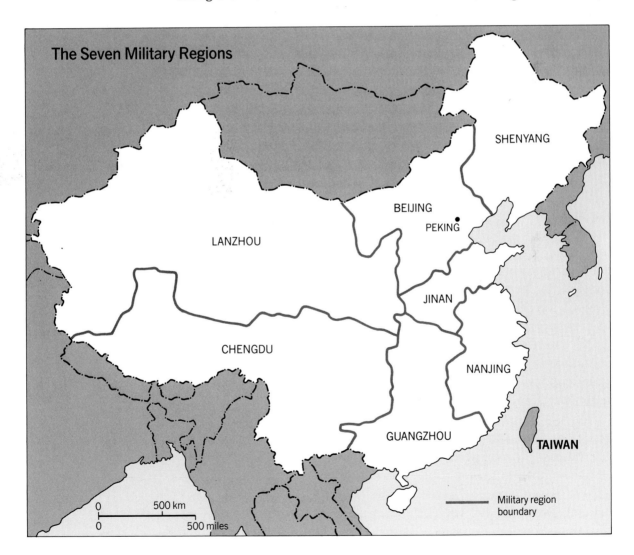

was not surprised when senior cadres within the Ministry of Defence refused, saying they were 'concerned for my safety'.

During the weeks we were together Mr Gu was always cautious when answering any of my questions. Obtaining information about the simplest matters relating to the military was exhausting – even on such elementary questions as pay and recruitment. Everything had to be referred to 'Our Leader' – a phrase I was to hear frequently during my time in China as a convenient way of deflecting the unwanted question.

Rarely did Mr Gu's personal life or feelings enter into our conversations, apart from his telling me one day that he was married with one child. By this time I was convinced that he was a senior cadre, regardless of his subtle attempts to deny it. We had been discussing the likelihood of the re-introduction of ranks in the PLA who have an 'on-off' attitude to this form of military grading. Finally we agreed that, in Western military terms, both he and Mr Chen would be colonels. His usual role within the Foreign Affairs Department at the Ministry of Defence was as interpreter for the better known international politicians and military leaders. Several weeks after my return to London we met on the steps of the Ministry of Defence. Resplendent in the dark olive green uniform of a PLA officer, he was acting as a senior aide and interpreter to China's Minister of Defence, General Zhang Aiping!

Special arrangements had been made for me to visit the Military Museum of the Chinese People's Revolution, situated on the north side of Fuxingmen Avenue, only a few minutes by car from the hotel where I was staying. This was an opportunity not to be missed, since few Westerners are allowed to visit the museum. Far from being elegant, it has a blockhouse style appearance, like so many other buildings in the area. The police guard at the gate stopped the car and peered in. After a few words, we were directed to a nearby parking space. Beside the entrance door, carved in white granite, stands a tri-service statue, showing the three components of the PLA (Army, Navy and Air Force). On the steps street vendors were selling soft drinks in long plastic tubes, along with sweets and food in crinkly packets.

Inside the museum's rotunda-like entrance stood a statue of Mao, also carved in white granite. Against the black background of the interior, it projected the very essence of the Helmsman of China, sombre, almost god-like. Beyond was a vast hall displaying all the paraphernalia of war. It had the feeling of some giant mausoleum dedicated to destruction and revolution. Dominating this amphitheatre of tanks, fieldguns and rocket-launchers was one

This giant military statue in granite outside the entrance to the museum on Fuxingmen Avenue depicts the three components of the PLA: the Army, the Navy and the Air Force.

of China's early space rockets, a slim, dart-like, silver object reaching up between the rounded girders of the chamber.

It occurred to me that there are times when we in the West tend to overlook the fact that China detonated her first atomic device more than twenty years ago, in October 1964: three years later, China exploded her first thermonuclear (hydrogen) bomb. Today, the PLA has the technology to deliver a warhead to a 8,000 target; her growing numbers of nuclear submarines can fire a strategic missile to reach an objective 2,500 miles away.

China's space programme is also well advanced, so much so that recently Western companies have been negotiating with China to launch their satellites. Understandably, the US government has certain misgivings and questions the wisdom of such undertakings

Many of the PLA's artillery and anti-aircraft weapons are over thirty years old; however, there are units still using weaponry similar to that displayed here.

The museum is an adventure playground for China's children!

until satisfied that the country's satellite technology will be safe from the prying eyes of the Chinese!

On an upper floor were galleries displaying the spoils of conflict: paintings and photographs of Red Army Generals, artefacts from the Long March and relics of the Japanese occupation. More showcases were packed with maps and diagrams of battles long forgotten except by a few remaining veterans. Here under one roof was the entire history of the People's Liberation Army. For the Chinese people this was a landscape where yesterday's warriors and heroes came to life.

One morning, I was taken on the most bizarre outing of my stay in Peking. It was into the underground tunnels of the city, built as air raid shelters back in the early sixties when the Chinese were alarmed by the possibility of attack from the Soviet Union.

Mr Chao, my guide, was a cheery middle-aged gentleman, who was an official in the local area. He told me that the whole city was connected by these passages with several hundred kilometres of them reaching out in all directions to the city's suburbs. The People's Liberation Army had been involved in their construction, supervizing the ordinary citizens who were responsible for the day-to-day construction. The section I was shown took over ten years to complete. When I asked how the building was done I was told: 'With our hands and simple tools.'

Tunnel entrances are in the most unusual places as I was soon to discover. On the corner of Dashalan Street, a narrow, busy thoroughfare reminiscent of old Peking, a small clothing shop was crowded with Wednesday afternoon shoppers. We stopped beside the first counter. On the left-hand side Mr Chao located a switch. Pressing it, the floor of the shop slid aside gently and silently, revealing a long flight of stairs leading down into a dimly-lit interior. It was evident that the sight of the floor sliding away surprised no one but myself, although maybe a few heads turned and looked at the Westerner descending into their civil defence system. At the bottom of the stairs another hidden switch was pressed, closing the floor above as silently as it had been opened. Peering into the gloom I saw that the tunnel beyond was no more than ten feet wide and perhaps twelve feet high. The air was damp and musty as we descended into a second gallery of passages. From time to time there were small notices along the walls; one of the largest of them was translated for me: 'Prepare Against War – Prepare Against Natural Disasters – Serve The People.' Mr Chao told me that this second floor went down to a depth of fifteen metres. Our steps and voices echoed along the passage, lit only by

89

During the late 1960s when the Chinese feared an impending Soviet invasion, a vast network of underground tunnels was constructed as part of a civil defence system. These tunnels were built by the local people assisted by the PLA. Entrances are cleverly concealed in various locations, including local shops.

the occasional bulb in the ceiling.

After a few minutes' walk the passage opened up into a much larger area leading to several spacious rooms. On the walls were a selection of photographs showing the tunnels' many uses. Following my guide, I was surprised to find myself in a large reception chamber. It must have been at least thirty feet long and half as wide, with chandeliered lighting, paintings and calligraphy on the walls, and comfortable chairs. 'This is used for banquets and parties,' Mr Chao explained. I was served tea while this part of the city's civil defences were described to me. 'You must understand that what you are going to see cannot be photographed,' my guide informed me politely. Pulling aside a small red curtain on the wall, he revealed a map showing this section of the complex: the exits, entrances, stairways, doors and the whole maze of connecting passageways leading to other parts of the system. Ordinarily, the Chinese authorities are reluctant to show foreigners anything of military significance. However, as the 'underground city' is on the tourist circuit and all the information on the map was in Chinese, my guide obviously felt there was little security risk in allowing me to see it.

An even greater surprise came when I discovered that various areas of the underground system had been commercialized. Exploring further I was taken to one of the many business enterprises, a large shop selling jade and porcelain to the tourist trade. Overhead strip lighting cast a greeny-blue hue, giving an almost supernatural atmosphere to this underground world. It was like a giant Aladdin's cave in a Christmas pantomime. A group of Japanese visitors drifted past, with only the slightest murmur, adding to the uncanny surroundings.

Surfacing into the crowded street it occurred to me that rather than return to my hotel by car, I could have asked my guide to take me there by way of the tunnels....

For that evening I had received an unexpected but very welcome invitation to dine with a senior cadre, Mr Zhan Maohai, the director of the European Section of the Foreign Affairs Bureau at the Defence Ministry. His area of interest, he told me during the

A large banqueting and conference hall within the underground complex. The government has commercialized sections of the network which includes hotels and shops.

evening, covered the USSR, the Warsaw Pact countries and Western Europe. In Whitehall terms, he would certainly have been classified as a Senior Civil Servant.

In retrospect I can see that our dinner was probably yet another informal screening process. There was little doubt in my mind after only a few days in Peking that as far as the Chinese were concerned, I was still 'on probation'. Dinner with Mr Zhan and his colleagues may well have been the final test before approval was granted for my visit.

Six of us sat down in the restaurant to dine.

Mr Zhan was tall, thin and spoke almost in a whisper. His quiet-spoken, perfect English demanded all my attention – which was, no doubt, what he intended. His piercing dark eyes behind glasses observed everything. Dressed in pale grey with an open-necked shirt, he could easily have passed for a trendy Jesuit.

It was obviously a popular eating spot for all the tables were full that evening. From the affluence of the clientele I realized that they were either part of China's growing business community or top-earning Party members and their friends. Instinctively, the

An underground shop catering to the tourist trade and selling ivory and lacquerware.

93

waiters knew Mr Zhan was to have the best service – and he got it. Beguiling Chinese girls glided around the table serving drinks and delicacies of Hung Shuo Yu (fish in brown sauce) and Xha Daxia (deep fried prawns) along with small bowls of delicious fish soup.

As might be expected, it was Mr Zhan who contributed most to the evening's conversation. 'I hope that you are happy with the arrangements that have been made for you,' he murmured. 'We are doing everything possible to fulfil your requests.'

We discussed Gadaffi's Libya and world terrorism, to which Mr Zhan commented: 'Our policy is quite clear on this: China is opposed to all forms of international terrorism, but at the same time, all people have a right to self-determination. Neither can we support any form of state terrorism.' When I asked him to elaborate, he smiled and declined.

On China's armed forces he was surprisingly frank. 'We are horribly behind, perhaps twenty years behind the West. It's in the area of technology that we are weakest. Cost is another thing,' he confided. China was aware of the high cost of Western technology; perhaps there could be a trade-off between China's rocket programme and the purchase of equipment from Europe and the United States....

Senior cadres, it appears, do not dally over dinner to the same extent as we do in Europe. No endless chatter over brandies and coffee. When the food had been eaten everyone departed. I had arrived at 6.30 pm and left a little after 8.30 pm. I never saw Mr Zhan again. Later I was informed that my programme had been approved and appropriate travel arrangements made.

3 The Achievers: Athletes, Sharpshooters and Generals

The PLA fighter is an excellent infantry soldier and sport plays an important part in his training routine.

In China sport has gone professional and is a highly competitive business. No longer are the days when the Chinese played for fun. For some reason the Chinese system of state support for its athletes – not unlike that in other Communist countries – is treated in an almost clandestine manner by the State Physical Culture and Sports Commission in Peking. Throughout China there are numerous sports schools and gyms where the country's potential future Olympic stars are sent. Another way to obtain a sports training is in the People's Liberation Army.

Sport and the military go very much hand in hand. There

A section of the out-dated barrack buildings of the August 1 Training Camp, with a sign welcoming friends from other countries.

At the August 1 Athletes' Training Camp outside Peking, PLA fighters loosen up before taking part in an early morning training run.

cannot be a military establishment anywhere, from the smallest jungle detachment to a famous military academy, that does not involve itself in some form of daily sporting activity, be it gymnastics, football or – as in China – table tennis and basketball.

As a prelude to visiting front line units of the People's Liberation Army, I was taken to the August 1 Sports Training Camp – the name of which commemorates the founding of the Red Army following the Nanchang uprising in 1927.

It was nearing mid-summer in Peking, with temperatures in the 80s and very high humidity, so I was delighted to be on my way

out of the city for the day. In the company of my two PLA minders, Mr Gu and Mr Chen, the driver of our air-conditioned Toyota lost no time in leaving the chaotic traffic of Fuxingmen Avenue behind.

This trip was to be my first glimpse of the Chinese countryside, so I was eager to absorb everything around me. We skirted Peking's industrial suburbs, with its iron, steel and petro-chemical plants. We drove north through the austere grey suburbs. Around us, partially-completed apartment blocks stood out like bleached skeletons on the skyline.

Though narrow, the road was a good one. We fought our way through an endless stream of farm traffic, and other hazards; donkeys, cattle, cyclists with mountainous loads – I never imagined a bicycle could carry so much, until I came to China – and scrawny chickens trying to escape our wheels.

Through the car window, I could see long lines of poplars, curving up and over us, making a giant gothic arch of trees. They went on endlessly, mile after mile. At the other side of the poplars were well-cultivated fields, worked by the villagers who were growing, I was told, mainly rice and grain. Ripening melons too, a profitable cash crop, would soon be ready for harvesting. Much to my surprise, I noticed that the dreary Mao suit of rough blue material, now a rare sight in the city, was also disappearing in the countryside in this part of China. The floppy-hatted peasants out there were tending the fruits of their newly-established free market; for the first time in many years they were working for personal profit.

Our destination turned out to be more than twenty miles from the city, and we arrived there in little over half an hour.

Surrounded by more tall poplars, the training camp was difficult to see from the road. Not only that, but there was little to show that this was a military area – even the sentry, a customary figure at most military establishments, was absent. As we drove through the entrance, it was indeed only the large sign in oversized white Chinese script against the red background which indicated to me that we had arrived.

At first sight, the away-from-it-all atmosphere seemed ideal. However, as a training centre for the PLA's Olympic hopefuls, the facilities here were far from adequate. The buildings were shabby and dilapidated, and there was not even a properly-equipped gymnasium, nor adequate showers or a swimming pool within the camp complex.

Not that these surprisingly poor training facilities seemed to have much effect on their performances. Their faces reflected that they had those qualities essential in every athlete: determination, aggression, and the desire to win.

Mr Chang, the PLA officer who ran the camp, agreed that facilities were not ideal, but claimed that things were improving. He pointed through the trees: already work had started on a new track and stadium. He told me that the athletes who came to the training camp had been selected by their units, after successfully competing in regimental events. 'They come here for a weekend, sometimes longer, to improve their technique. If they are successful, they will go on to compete at a higher level. It is even possible that they could represent China.' Could it be that I was seeing some of China's future Olympic sportsmen and women, I asked him. He smiled and replied: 'Quite possible.'

Around the dirt track behind me, the weekend intake of PLA athletes was limbering up. Stretching, pulling and grunting, one group near me put in a determined effort before lining up for the start of a cross-country event, while at the far corner of the track, other athletes worked at their exercises alone, more like ballet dancers at the barre, making slow graceful shapes with their arms, legs and bodies. At regular intervals, the starter set off the next cross-country runner. It was a long course but all of them set out at a scorching pace, turned left under the entrance arch, and out for the long run into the open countryside.

Meanwhile from behind the mess hall came the intermittent crack of small bore weapons. On the steps outside the indoor range two women in coloured tee-shirts and green army slacks were busily cleaning their small bore sports pistols. Once inside, I saw in the dim light that the single-storied building contained several shooting galleries. The one I had entered was open to the daylight at the far end, illuminating the small cardboard targets. A dozen or so young people were participating, using various models of sports pistols, vintage by European standards. Everyone wore ear protectors and from time to time they would check the placing of their shots through small spotting scopes.

Each competitor was in his own small cubicle, which minimized unwanted outside distractions. Behind me, one of the young marksmen adopted various postures, raising and lowering his pistol at the wall. These were the young men and women of the People's Liberation Army, who prefer to be called fighters rather than soldiers. Here they were shooting as sportsmen, but there is little doubt that the skills learnt here at the August 1 Camp could easily be transferred to the assault rifle and machine-gun.

From a discreet distance I watched a woman dressed in an blue sweatshirt and olive green army trousers prepare to shoot.

An early arrival in the morning cross-country run at the August 1 Training Camp.

In addition to an intensive athletic programme the men and women undergo further training in sports pistol and rifle shooting. Although many of the weapons are dated this does not reduce the enthusiasm and determination of these young marksmen and women or detract from their skills. If they succeed in gaining high scores they will be recommended for further training. Some of them may well be representing the People's Republic of China in a future Olympic Games.

She slipped a fresh magazine into the butt of the pistol, shuffled her feet into the right stance and concentrated on the floor for a few seconds. Slowly, she raised the pistol to the aim in a two-handed grip. Firing rapidly in bursts of two, she emptied the magazine, making a neat grouping in the cardboard target, twenty-five metres down range. With accuracy and cool professional determination, the exercise was completed in a few seconds.

When I enquired how many women were serving in the PLA the Chinese were unwilling to commit themselves. At a rough estimate, I suspect that there are several thousand, between the

In their modest dining hall the athletes are provided with a healthy, well-balanced diet comprising fish soup, raw vegetables with chicken and rice, fresh fruit and soft drinks.

Army, Navy and the Air Force. Then there is the militia, in which women play a very active role. Accounts from PLA archives indicate that although there were only some thirty women cadres with the main army of the Long March, working mainly as porters and medical orderlies, in the Fourth Front Army there was a special women's combat regiment which fought with some distinction. I was interested, therefore, to know if the PLA today trained their women to be combat troops, or even taught them to use the Kalashnikov assault rifle. During the course of the morning I discussed this with Mr Chang and he told me that women were only trained in administrative and nursing duties. This surprised me since only a few days previously, I had been presented with a book, in which there were illustrations showing Chinese women in smart blue uniforms, complete with white trilby hats and matching gloves, armed with the latest Kalashnikov, marching as part of a large contingent through Tiananmen Square. I had been told that they were members of the People's Militia.

Lunch time arrived. The interior of the mess hall was modest, clean and bright. A long screen divided the hall into two sections. Other than for decoration, it seemed to serve no useful purpose. Perhaps there was some sort of seniority in the mess, with the screen as the demarcation line, but I was not told about it. On each side was a neat line of round tables covered with clean white tablecloths. Seating was on small tubular stools. There was plenty to eat for everyone. Every table had several dishes of meat, fish, soup and blown white bread rolls, looking like oversize marshmallows. In spite of their lunchtime banter, the young fighter-athletes managed to eat their food in double-quick time. Afterward, everyone washed their own plates in a long trough at the far end of the dining hall. As they left, most of them helped themselves to an apple from a large barrel by the door.

A table had been specially set aside for our party in a corner, giving me an excellent view of the mess. Like the other tables, ours was crowded with a delightful assortment of food; from fish soup to chunks of chicken in rice. It was easy to see where I was expected to sit; one of the places had a spoon and fork placed beside the chopsticks. Mr Gu, my interpreter, was already discovering some of my eating problems, along with my likes and dislikes.

There was a time in Communist China when all sporting activities were purely recreational – a relief from the monotony of factory and farm production. Winning was not the prime reason for playing or participating. Today China's athletes are highly-motivated and they are out to win! As it trains its fighters to defend the

Many of the female athletes prefer to eat at their own table. After lunch the athletes wash their own dishes at a large washing area, located at one end of the mess hall. Living accommodation is primitive compared to quarters provided for British Forces athletes undergoing similar training programmes.

Motherland, so the PLA will make a major contribution in training China's athletes to compete in the international sporting arena.

Higher education for all ranks, especially the officer corps, is one of the most recent important developments within China's military. Later that week I was taken to see the PLA's first military university.

Two years ago many of the PLA's officers would have graduated from the Military Academy at Shrijiazhuang, a city some three hours' drive away to the south of Peking. It was one of the leading training centres for the military in China. Now this has changed. China's future generals and marshals are trained at the newly-inaugurated (1986) National Defence University of the People's Liberation Army, the country's foremost centre for military studies, incorporating the former PLA Military Academy, the PLA Political Academy and the PLA Logistics Academy. The veteran General Zhang Zhen is now the President.

The People's Liberation Army is overburdened with elderly generals of the old military school. There are still a tiny number of serving leaders who are veterans of the Long March of more than fifty years ago. One of the founders of the PLA, Marshall Liu Bocheng, nicknamed the 'One-Eyed Dragon', did not retire from active service until he was ninety years old! Younger officers are quietly murmuring that these ageing fighters should be pensioned off, retired, to give the younger men the opportunity of promotion. Many officers, feeling that for years it has been a question of waiting to fill dead men's shoes, are now leaving the PLA, in the hope of establishing themselves within China's new free enterprise economy. Among younger members of the Party too, there are those who criticize the eighty-three year old Deng Xiaoping for retaining power for so long; Deng has absolute control of the military through the Party's Military Commission and the Central Military Commission. But it was Deng himself who gave official endorsement for the retirement of old PLA faithfuls in 1985, when he announced that one million officers and men would be released. There was an added purpose to this: to demonstrate to the world that China wished to follow the path of peace – especially in South-East Asia. In the past China's Military Region Commanders had been accused of imposing a style of authority throughout their commands not unlike that of the despotic warlords of China's past. Now, with the reorganization of the PLA there is a new breed of commander, who is hoping that the strongly Maoist old sweats will quietly disappear, like twigs in the flowing waters of the Yangtze.

Everyone in China is encouraged to regard themselves as 'Fighters for the Motherland'. Deng has reminded them, furthermore, that the days are over when all a fighter needed before going into battle was a rifle, a bayonet, some grenades, and tofu. The PLA's leaders are fully aware that it is not only knowledge, but hi-tech knowledge, that is important to this new generation of soldiers.

Nestling at the foot of the Western Hills – you arrive there in under an hour by car from Peking – the white stone buildings of the National Defence University sprawl campus-style among pleasant trees and flower beds. On my arrival I was met by Captain Yang Jun, my interpreter for the visit, who spoke excellent English.

I was immediately whisked into the congenial atmosphere of that sort of briefing room which has soft easy chairs and the latest overhead projector. In overall command of the students at the new Defence University was Colonel Fan Zhicai. This was the first time that I had heard a Western rank ascribed to a PLA officer. My interpreter, Mr Yang, indicated to me that in our Western forces his

The National Defence University is situated in the western hills near Peking. The campus has an air of seclusion about it. It was officially opened in early 1986 and that September six hundred students commenced their studies here.

There is a bright, contemporary feel about the interior of the library building at the National Defence University. The flag on display is a replica of that of the Japanese Resistance University which was established in the former Communist stronghold of Northern Shaanxi.

rank would be equivalent to that of a captain.

Ranks are a delicate subject at the Ministry of Defence these days. No one wishes to commit themselves as to when the rank system finally will be reintroduced. 'Sometime – perhaps next year,' is the reply of some senior cadres. Without doubt, there is a definite downplaying of the subject by the military. Once-powerful cadres and commissars, who participated in the Cultural Revolution, and still have influence within the conservative elements of the Party, currently oppose the implementation of the newly-legalized rank system – a system that some believe could bring about an élitist officer corps within the People's Liberation Army.

For the next half an hour, surrounded by a number of officers from the university, I was treated to a detailed 'teach in' on the new establishment. From time to time flow charts were projected onto a large screen; while at my side Captain Yang interpreted everything in enormous detail. It was all quite overwhelming – as I am sure it was meant to be.

Courses could be from six months to three years. After the three-year course the student would receive a degree. Science subjects of every description were prominent, together with a balanced amount of Marxist-Leninist political study.

Colonel Fan, the students' commanding officer, elaborated the four main policies of the university for me. 'We are here,' he said, 'to promote friendship, our open door policy, all round training, and the streamlining of our forces.' Such predictable Communist

Throughout the ranks of the PLA education plays an important part in the military's modernization programme. At the University of Defence, the leading military education institution in China, middle-ranking officers attend courses in new disciplines such as computer sciences and information technology.

As many of the elderly PLA officers are being retired, middle-ranking officers, who will one day become the future marshals and generals of the PLA, are now sent to the National Defence University.

propaganda was only to be expected from within China's highest military institute.

'I am afraid there are very few students here at the moment, as our term does not begin until September. This will be our first term and we are expecting at least six hundred students,' Captain Yang told me.

During the next hour, I was steered through large and small lecture halls with their television monitors and projection screens; visited a library still being filled with books and watched middle-ranking male officers being lectured on computers by female instructors.

Perhaps the PLA would be reluctant to admit it, but it is going back to basics and evaluating itself, in the light of current technology and modern warfare. Clearly the Military is eager to compensate for lost time and is setting a course for the twenty-first century, which combines providing a hi-tech education for its officers with the appropriate weapons for its fighters.

4 Strauss Chinese Style: The Band of the PLA

As we British know, there's nothing better than a good brass band to attract the crowds and get the folks humming. From Bridlington and Brighton to the leafy parks of London, locals and tourists alike respond to the Oom-Pah-Pah of a good military band. Surely there can be no better way of spending an idle lunch hour on a warm summer's day than munching cucumber sandwiches to the sound of the Band of the Irish Guards.

The same applies in China. And now once again, after the upheavals of the Cultural Revolution, the Chinese are able to appreciate the rousing music of the military band. In fact everything musical is a crowd puller these days in Peking.

It should be remembered that during the Cultural Revolution all the arts were seen as representing Western influence and degeneracy, and therefore rejected. China entered a period of artistic depression; the country became a cultural wilderness. It was a period of national anguish that was to last for over ten years, during which performances of Western music would have been unthinkable. Some musicians would have been dispatched to remote villages to work in the fields – and these would have been the fortunate ones. Others would just disappear, spirited away by the notorious Red Guards, never to be seen again.

This purge of the nation's culture was the obsession of Mao's wife, the infamous Jiang Qing, one-time actress and filing clerk in Mao's office. Through slick power play she managed to manoeuvre her way to become China's Cultural Director. Jiang Qing conducted a reign of terror against China's writers, film-makers and musicians – in fact, everybody who represented the nation's culture.

So it was with considerable interest one evening that I attended a concert given by the band of the People's Liberation Army. Imagine: the one-time guardians of the Cultural Revolution now performing the works of Strauss and Puccini! Here was a change indeed.

The band was playing at the People's Theatre, an auditorium in Huguosi, a district in the western part of Peking. It was a packed

It is not unusual when the band is practising near home for the members' families to come and listen to them play. The musicians of the People's Liberation Army Band, like military bands the world over, travel a great deal (throughout China) and are given enthusiastic welcomes wherever they perform.

113

house; well over 1,500 people had come to listen to the PLA concert.

Before the concert began, I had a chance to chat with the conductor, Mr Liu Yubao, who was also the Director of Music. In a spacious room beside the stage, we discussed the band and the evening's concert. In the background, musicians tinkered with their instruments and unpacked music.

Mr Liu would be in his early fifties. Slightly grey at the temples, he was wearing gold-rimmed glasses and his face had the happy, contented expression of a man at peace with the world. As it was a warm evening, and the concert an informal one, he and the band wore only their white open-necked shirts and olive green service trousers.

Born in Jiangxi Province, Mr Liu had taken up music as a boy when he was fourteen years old, and his parents had sent him to train at music schools in Peking and Shanghai. Forty years ago, when China was embroiled in a savage civil war, can hardly have been the best of times for a family to put a son through musical training; but they managed it somehow.

Music and the Arts have enjoyed an overwhelming resurgence in recent years, in total contrast to the years of the Cultural Revolution when participation in any cultural pursuit was considered decadent. The PLA, who once helped to sustain these radical policies, are now helping to create a new artistic climate in China.

114

Although, even as a boy, his main love had been the piano, over the years he had learnt to play several instruments, including the saxophone and clarinet. He took a little persuading before he would reveal to me his great passion for composition. But in the past he had composed several pieces for the band, and shyly he was delighted to admit that, yes, they were popular whenever they were played.

He had travelled all over China with the band, he told me, but as yet there had been no opportunity for him to travel out of the country to experience music in other parts of the world. I commiserated with him, saying that I hoped this would soon change.

Between endless orange drinks, we discussed brass bands in Britain and his eyes sparkled when I told him of our works bands with their annual festivals and competitions. He was aware of Britain's brass band tradition and had managed to hear recorded music of our military bands. When we discussed instruments, not surprisingly, he was unaware that Britain produced some of the finest band instruments in the world. Would China consider

The People's Liberation Army has about four hundred musicians divided into four bands with between eighty to a hundred musicians in each, depending on the function at which they are performing.

115

buying instruments from Britain, I enquired. He spread out his hands and smiled. Like bands the world over it was a question of funds. They too were short of cash.

The new Communist regime in China was only in its infancy when the PLA band was first formed in 1952. Nevertheless a recruiting procedure has been adopted by the authorities to ensure a steady flow of musical talent. There are two ways a young man or woman can enter. Either as a cadet musician, who after four years' training will join the band as a junior musician, or as a graduate of China's music schools. Women are still very much in the minority – the only one I recall seeing in the band was the harpist.

Until recently, there were about seven hundred musicians in the PLA. But these are hard times for musicians all over the world and Communist China is no exception. The result: some three hundred musicians have recently been made redundant. However, there may now be a more positive approach on the horizon: during 1986 forty students were accepted for training. Perhaps the lay-offs were in fact a way of rejuvenating the PLA's musical talent. . . .

Currently the four hundred remaining musicians are divided between four main bands, with eighty to one hundred musicians in each, depending on the occasion. Playing for visiting dignitaries seems to be one of the main roles of the PLA's musicians these days in the capital. Between the four bands, they travel a great deal within China. No doubt music carries the PLA flag into the more remote regions, underlining to the people that the army is still very much in command. At the same time, it shows that there is a lighter side to military life back in the power-house that is Peking.

There was the usual assortment of instruments in the band: trumpets, bassoons, piccolos, tubas, and such like. When I remarked on the number of clarinetists – there were fourteen playing with the band – Mr Liu replied: 'It is a lovely instrument, such a beautiful sound.'

On stage the brass and woodwinds were practising scales. The double bass player plucked away at a few bars with the rhythm of a jazz player, while the percussionist strummed his fingers across a small side drum, listened, then made a small adjustment. Down in the auditorium the audience was becoming restless, anxious for the concert to begin. Mr Liu looked at his watch and pulled a face. 'It is time for the concert to start; I hope you enjoy our music.'

Arrangements had been made for me to stay back-stage, where there would be better opportunities to photograph, and at the same time observe the musicians at close range. I knew Mr Liu had reached the stage by the genteel clap of the crowd, certainly a less

The band has many applicants: most come by way of a cadet musician training programme, or from a recognized school of music. When they enter the band they will be under the close supervision of the Director of Music, Mr Liu Yubao, and one of the senior instrumentalists.

lusty reception than would be heard in a British concert hall. But from the wings I had an excellent view of Mr Liu conducting and was also able to move from one side of the stage to the other without being seen from the auditorium.

While it may be the custom – depending on the occasion – for a Western concert to open with a country's national anthem, to have the anthems of several countries played as an opening number would be considered slightly unusual by Western concert-goers. But not in Peking. The opening piece was a medley of anthems, played with verve and aplomb. The hall echoed to the anthems of the United States, France, West Germany, Russia and others that I

Mr Liu Yubao of the PLA conducts at an evening concert in Peking. As it is hot he allows the band to play without wearing full military uniform. He expressed a wish to come to Britain to experience some of the British Military Band traditions.

118

did not recognize. Among these were Romania and other Eastern Bloc countries, I was told later.

The audience lost no time in showing their praise. As soon as the final notes were played and Mr Liu turned round and gave a long, gracious bow, the audience showed their approval with a mixture of vigorous clapping and appreciative shouts. Clearly an encore was needed. With a flourish of his baton, Mr Liu needed no further encouragement. A delighted audience sat back and were given not one, or even two of the anthems – but the entire selection!

The PLA musicians played with delightful enthusiasm. It was obvious that they particularly enjoyed the popular tunes of Strauss, Puccini and Verdi. The literal bounce of the conductor was a joy to watch. The audience missed no opportunity to clap and cheer. Listening to the music at the back of the stage brought on a touch of home-sickness, something I had rarely experienced during many years of foreign assignments. But this was China – this was another world. The West seemed a million miles away.

During the interval I chatted with Mr Liu about the performance. There had been rapturous applause for one particular piece of music. 'What was the name of it?' I asked him.

'That is a very popular piece of music wherever we go, especially in the countryside. We call it: *The Happy News Has Reached The Remote Village*.' On the thirtieth anniversary of the founding of the People's Republic, the band won first prize when they played the piece in a competition. The title I would always remember; the tune, however, was not exactly one you could hum as you left the concert hall!

Perhaps, even so, a few summers from now, the strains of *The Happy News Has Reached The Remote Village* will pour out from the bandstands of Bridlington and Brighton? That would be happy news indeed....

5 With the Peking Third Garrison Division

China has the largest fighting force in the world. The People's Liberation Army was born out of revolution and its fighters are regarded as the sons and daughters of the people. Collectively, China's total military strength is overwhelming: at very short notice, seventeen million men and women can be summoned to fight for the Motherland. This includes the main and regional ground forces of the PLA, the Air Force and Navy, together with numerous paramilitary units. At present the PLA is undergoing internal political reforms and a modernization programme which will have far reaching effects, not only in South-East Asia, but throughout the whole Western world.

China has a compulsory military service programme, but it is highly selective: from the several millions of young people reaching the conscription age of eighteen each year, only an estimated three-quarters of a million are accepted for training. Until recently, recruit training was unstructured and took place within the active service regiment. Now things are different; recruits are being trained on Western lines, at specialized training establishments. This also applies to NCO and specialist training courses. The conscript who is drafted into the army serves for a three-year period. The Navy has recently increased its period of enlistment from four to five years, while the Air Force requirement still remains four years. All may re-enlist if the needs of the particular service demand it.

China would like everyone to believe that the post-Maoist PLA is smaller in numbers than it really is. On more than one occasion, whilst I was with them, senior officers and political commissars would make a point of telling me about their contraction programme. More than a million personnel were being released from the armed services and when this was complete, they said the PLA would be under three million. I have my doubts: most Western sources suggest a figure nearer to three and a half million, organized into some thirty-five armies supported by thirteen armoured, seventeen artillery and several airborne divisions and,

The PLA has now adopted Western-style head-dress throughout the three branches of the armed services. However, in a working situation some units are wearing the old-style 'liberation hat'.

according to my information, this is still a conservative estimate. It would be far more realistic to say that China's regular forces including her conscripts exceed five million – and this is taking into account the 'golden handshake' programme that is currently in progress for veteran generals and senior officers. Add to that number the millions of trained militia scattered throughout the country, and you have a formidable armed force, a force far greater than that of the USSR. Regardless of the current overtures being made by the Soviets to Peking, following a period of strained relations lasting more than a quarter of a century, China is still highly suspicious of her northern neighbour. Border incidents between the two countries have occurred in the past, but nothing too serious recently. Nevertheless, as far as the Chinese are concerned, the Russians are a constant threat.

There was a time in the 1950s when Russia's influence with China was thought to be a strong and lasting one; and with some city architecture this is still in evidence today. Russian was China's second language, too, for a time but with the dissolution of the Soviet Alliance, the educational needs of the people have changed. Now everyone in China is eager to learn English. The intention of the Soviets was to convert China into a Russian satellite; when China resisted, the Russians withdrew all their support and aid programmes. From then on, the Chinese followed their natural instinct and moved towards national isolationism and set out to build a new wall around themselves, with particular emphasis on their defence policy.

Inevitably China has paid dearly for her self-imposed isolation and the calamitous error of the Cultural Revolution. Now in this new age of the so-called Liberal Open Door, China's leaders are willing to admit that in certain aspects the PLA is antiquated, and that its generals and senior commanders are beginning to resent the limited provision of modern equipment. However, the Chinese are facing a dilemma: their armed forces require large amounts of foreign exchange with which to purchase Western hardware and technology, but of the four modernizations proposed by the Party, defence is the last. How China will resolve this difficulty remains to be seen. Broadly speaking, until recently the PLA has done little since the Soviet-dominated early fifties to improve its weaponry: the Infantry, for example, are still using their home-produced equivalent of the Soviet SKS 7.62 Simonov semi-automatic rifle. There are similar examples throughout the PLA, from Russian-based artillery designs to the Air Force's adaptation of MiG 19s; even the Navy has a strong Soviet character

Army Dispositions

Shenyang (north-east)	Chengdu (south-west)
5 armoured divisions	15 infantry divisions
23 infantry divisions	6 regional forces+
13 regional forces+	1 missile
2 missiles	
	Guangzhou (south)
Beijing (north)	16 infantry divisions
4 armoured divisions	12 regional forces+
25 infantry divisions	
1 airborne (Airforce)	Jinan (centre)
13 regional forces	2 armoured divisions
1 missile	10 infantry divisions
	3 airborne (Airforce)
Lanzhou (west)	6 regional forces
1 armoured division	
13 infantry divisions	Nanjing (east)
9 regional forces+	1 armoured division
2 missiles	16 infantry divisions
	14 regional forces

Land forces

Main air base

Missiles

* Statistical information taken from
The Military Balance, ITSS, London

+ denotes that there are 2-3 divisions worth
of border troops in these Military Regions

about it, from frigates to submarines. Newly-designed uniforms have replaced the green pyjama-like outfit of the Maoist era, but they still have a distinct Russian look about them.

There are signs, however, of a deep and significant change in the PLA's weaponry. The Infantry has already started feeding into its system a limited quantity of the new 5.56 semi-automatic rifle, which is not unlike the American M16 in performance. Anti-tank weapons, always a weakness with the PLA in the past, have now been updated and other much needed hardware, including minelayers, multiple rocket launchers and mortars, is currently more widely available to PLA units, along with an improved 60 mm anti-tank rifle grenade capable of piercing several inches of armour plating. To relieve the footsore infantry and give them greater mobility, strategically important units are now equipped with armoured personnel carriers (APCs) one of which has been developed in Britain in co-operation with the Chinese arms manufacturer Norinco. According to certain Western sources, the Navy is reported to be developing a new twenty thousand ton aircraft carrier. However, when the Chinese Ministry of Defence gave their first ever press conference in Peking recently, Xu Xin, Deputy Chief of the General Staff of the PLA, denied that such a project was in progress.

I had been invited to spend some time with the PLA's Third Garrison Division in Shunyi County, some fifty miles to the north-east of Peking. There were, I was told, roughly thirteen thousand troops in the division, including a regiment of artillery.

In China's military history, this division is a famous one, with a long pedigree of battle honours and celebrated names. It was founded in 1927, and is therefore one of the oldest units in the PLA. Out of the 1927 Nanchang Uprising, the Red Army, the forerunner of today's PLA, was born. The uprising itself was a disaster; an ambitious idea that ended in bitter failure, but it would not be the first time in history that out of the ashes of failure victory emerged. Preserving its sense of history, the division still has seventeen companies which can trace their origins to this time. Two of the PLA's most revered commanders during the Red Army period were closely associated with this unit: Marshals Chen Yi and Chu Teh.

All my equipment fitted neatly in the car's boot – with the exception of my film stock, which was placed beside me on the rear seat. It made a comfortable arm rest as I settled back in the corner of the air-conditioned Nissan.

We left Peking after an early breakfast; I had been warned that there was a busy day ahead as a full programme had been planned at the Third Garrison Division. It was just after 7.30 as we drove out of the hotel courtyard; the morning rush hour was building up, the buses were packed and the cycle lane moved in one continuous line – a stream of flowing cycles.

There was no respite in the hot steamy weather although, glancing skywards now that we were clear of the Peking smog, I could see that the sky was blue, and the light was bright and contrasty. Still, the car interior was cool, and the bespectacled young man who was driving us handled the Nissan with great skill, zipping along the long lines of buses and muddy-green Liberation

When we were nearing a military establishment a motor-cycle and side-car outrider would lead the way; on entering the military compound we would be given further directions by a PLA flagman.

trucks which were also heading northwards at alarming speeds.

From time to time during our travels together, my interpreter Mr Gu would talk to me about the complexities of the English language. Although his English was excellent, there was always some nuance of the language he liked to discuss. On one of these occasions I spent a great deal of time trying to clarify the phrase a 'political banana skin'. Another was far more complex, involving the phrase 'political middle ground'. Trying to explain this

A tough infantry officer, Mr Liu Yi Ming is Deputy Commander of Peking's Third Garrison Division. 'Let us drink to the peace of our two countries,' he said to me over lunch.

particular democratic stance to a Communist can be a problem, and I must admit I have reservations as to the degree of my success. But these discussions were useful to me. I felt they created obligation and therefore bargaining power, so that when I came to ask for something or other during the course of the day, my request was more likely to be at least considered, rather than simply dismissed out of hand.

Ahead of us I could see the familiar sludgy-green uniform of a PLA soldier standing in the middle of the road, signalling for us to turn left. As we passed he stood stiffly to attention, his arms fully extended at right angles. In each hand a small flag fluttered in the breeze – one red, the other green. We followed the direction of the extended green flag a hundred or so yards down the road, until another flagman turned us through a pair of gates and into a small courtyard with a large ornamental rock formation in the centre. On the steps of one of the two-storied buildings surrounding the courtyard, several officers in open-necked summer uniform awaited our arrival.

Everyone shook hands and smiled. Along with the other officers in the welcoming party, Mr Liu Yi Ming, the Deputy Commander of the Peking Third Garrison Division, picked up a piece of my baggage and ushered me up the short flight of steps into the building.

As I passed through the coloured plastic strips hung to make a screen over the entrance, the two soldiers standing on either side flicked a smart salute. They wore white cotton gloves which gave an added touch of crispness to the gesture. A small suite had been set aside for me on the first floor, comprising a sitting room, a bedroom, and a rather sad-looking bathroom that certainly needed a coat of paint, as well as several replacement tiles around the bath. Two sizeable sofas took up most of the sitting room, along with the low table and television set in the far corner. The bedroom next to it had a large double bed, with an assortment of blankets and a hard pillow which felt as if it were packed with straw, and a small table-type desk by the open window. A mosquito net was draped over the bed, supported by a simple canopy of thin bamboo sticks.

All my photographic equipment and baggage had been piled into a corner by the door. The accommodation was far better than I had expected. Comfort was the last thing I needed, and I would have gladly slept in a draughty earth-floored barrack block if necessary. I went into the bedroom and tested the mattress. It was firm and comfortable. As I peered out of the window and watched the peasants cutting corn in the field at the other side of the dirt

127

farm road, I wondered which cadre or officer had been asked to give up his accommodation on my behalf.

'The Deputy Commander wishes to welcome you. Would you come this way?' I followed Mr Gu downstairs into a large reception room, furnished with the same brown easy chairs and lace accessories on the arms and headrests that you see in every hotel room in China. We sat facing each other across the room, about fifteen feet apart. Mr Liu sat with a senior officer on either side of him. Mr Gu began interpreting. 'Mr Liu and his officers wish to welcome you to the Beijing Third Garrison Division. He says that it is an honour for them that you have come to visit and they hope your stay will increase the friendship between our two countries.' While all this was going on, two soldiers entered, one with cold face flannels, the other carrying a tray of bottled orange juice, which was opened and poured into glasses on the table before us.

It intrigued me that there was so much distance between us during our discussions. Was this perhaps a symbolic demonstration of the subtle isolationism still present in China? Seated there at the far end of the room, between his two subordinates, Mr Liu certainly gave the appearance of a traditional warlord. There was a dominating presence about him. He was built like an ox and his square face, close-cropped hair and meaty hands gave him an almost ruthless appearance. Even his occasional chortle had a sinister ring. He had served in the PLA for twenty-five years, which meant that he had been in the army five years at the time of the Cultural Revolution. He told me that he might be retiring soon and returning to his home town, Tianjin City. Then as I sipped the orange and wiped my hands and face again with the cold facecloth, he described some of the places I would be seeing.

A visit had been arranged to the nearby divisional museum, their hospital and medical facilities. That evening there was to be a basketball game in the camp. Later, if I wished, I could visit some of the soldiers in their barracks. I expressed my appreciation. Mr Liu continued: 'We will also take you to see a company of our Infantry in training, then our Artillery Regiment, and finally our Tank Division.' He flashed a large smile as he concluded. We all strolled over to the museum in one of the buildings across the courtyard.

Mao's quotation over the entrance proclaimed that 'A Single Spark Can Start A Prairie Fire'. The museum itself was well designed and packed with the usual memorabilia of war. A wall-size multicoloured flow chart outlined the various campaigns in which the Division had taken part. A scratchy recording with music and English soundtrack accompanied the illuminated lines

At every military establishment that I visited a familiar ritual took place: there would be endless discussions regarding my needs and expectations accompanied by cold flannels, liberal servings of China tea and orange squash, served by PLA stewards. Listening to my requests is Mr Liu Yi Ming, assisted by his political commissar and a senior officer of the regiment.

and flashing lights, but did little to improve my understanding.

During the Korean War, in which members of the regiment participated, political expediency had dictated that they be referred to as 'Volunteers'. A prolonged involvement in Korea was never anticipated by the Chinese since, at that time, they were contemplating invading Taiwan, but heavy US naval presence in the area deterred them. Now, more than thirty years later, and in spite of the losses which Chinese 'Volunteers' sustained, China still vigorously justifies having become embroiled in the Korean conflict. In forthright terms the curator spoke of the regiment's contribution in Korea. They went, he said, to help annihilate the Imperialists, who had invaded the area. In the climate of China's ostensibly liberal attitudes towards the West, I was surprised to hear the PLA still maintain such outspoken anti-Imperialist attitudes.

We all went to lunch which was a grand and sumptuous affair. Ten of us gathered at a very large circular table, around which a large screen had been positioned. It gave me the feeling of being in a giant Chinese restaurant! I had hoped to have been taken into the fighters' mess, to see how the lower ranks were fed, but instead I

129

was getting the 'high table' treatment. The table was laden with a dozen or more plates of food, everything from cucumber slices with chilli to fresh fish in soy and chilli sauce, along with rice and clear fish soup. As colourful as it looked, it was not for me, so I helped myself to a few simple things: chicken slices, tomatoes, and such like. Once again a knife and spoon had been thoughtfully provided.

There was plenty to drink, including the fiery and intoxicating Maotai from South-West China, made from millet and sorghum. My stomach decidedly unsettled, I drank a toast to the friendship of our two countries in orange juice. It was one of several toasts during the course of the meal; there were others to the peace of the world, the officers and soldiers of the Division, and the Veterans of the Long March. Plenty of lively banter was exchanged between two of the officers, deputy commanders, who had not seen each other for some time. By now the Maotai was flowing quite freely. Every so often Mr Liu – who was by now quite jolly – would chink my glass and toast: 'Friendship to our two countries', to which I would solemnly reply: 'Friendship to our two countries'.

After lunch I was glad to rest for an hour in the cool of my room, away from the heat of the midday sun. There was time to unpack and prepare equipment for the afternoon visit to the PLA hospital.

We went by car even though it was only a short distance across the dusty parade square. We passed rows of drab single-storey barracks that went on as far as the eye could see – it was only the poplars that brought a touch of relief along the narrow connecting roads. We passed what appeared to be a newly-constructed

Sleeping accommodation for the PLA fighter is modest compared to that of many Western armies. Personal, toilet and washing utensils are arranged in military fashion in one corner of the dormitory. Washing and toilet facilities would be outside and there certainly is no running hot water in these barracks!

130

A young PLA fighter strums away, spending his evenings teaching himself to play the guitar, while his friends play table tennis and a form of billiards.

The Chinese fighter is unpaid, although he is given a small monthly allowance for such things as soap and writing materials. All food and uniforms are issued free of charge. In certain cases a family support allowance is allowed if the recruit's absence from home is causing hardship. Without money to spend, the young men and women of the PLA spend a great deal of time entertaining themselves in the barrack blocks.

131

headquarters building on our right, with a cluster of communications antennae on the roof.

We parked the car at the hospital gate and walked the last few
yards to the main entrance. Above us, on the first floor, some of the
patients poked their heads through the windows to see the
foreigner. We waved to each other.

There was quite a crowd inside to welcome us. After meeting
many people and having endless photographs taken by the two
PLA photographers, Mr Gu and I, and about a dozen officials set out
to tour the hospital. Even in the cool interior I still felt hot. Small
rivulets of perspiration dribbled down my face which I wiped away
with the towelling sweatband around my wrist.

The PLA's medical services and hospitals not only serve the
military, but the local population as well. Contrary to my expec-
tation, I was told that the service was not free to non-military
personnel and that, if they could afford to, civilian patients were
expected to pay a small fee. As many as fifty per cent of the patients
being treated at any one time by the PLA would be non-military.
British military hospitals have a similar commitment to the National
Health Service, though the percentage of civilian patients in, say,

Preparing natural medicines
in the hospital dispensary at
the Peking Third Garrison
Division and, below, the
pharmacist.

China's flourishing bicycle industry had no doubt contributed towards this contemporary piece of equipment in the hospital's small physiotherapy department. All the doctors at the PLA hospital were trained in both Western and traditional forms of medicine.

Aldershot Military Hospital would be nowhere near as high.

While I was in China I was told about an outstanding operation carried out by a PLA medical team at the Number Four Medical College in Shaanxi Province. Wang Futao, a twenty-year-old industrial worker, lost all her fingers at work. A paper-cutting machine had sliced them all off at their base. She was rushed to hospital, the fingers wrapped in rags. There, a team of twenty-six doctors and medical workers worked for twenty-seven hours to

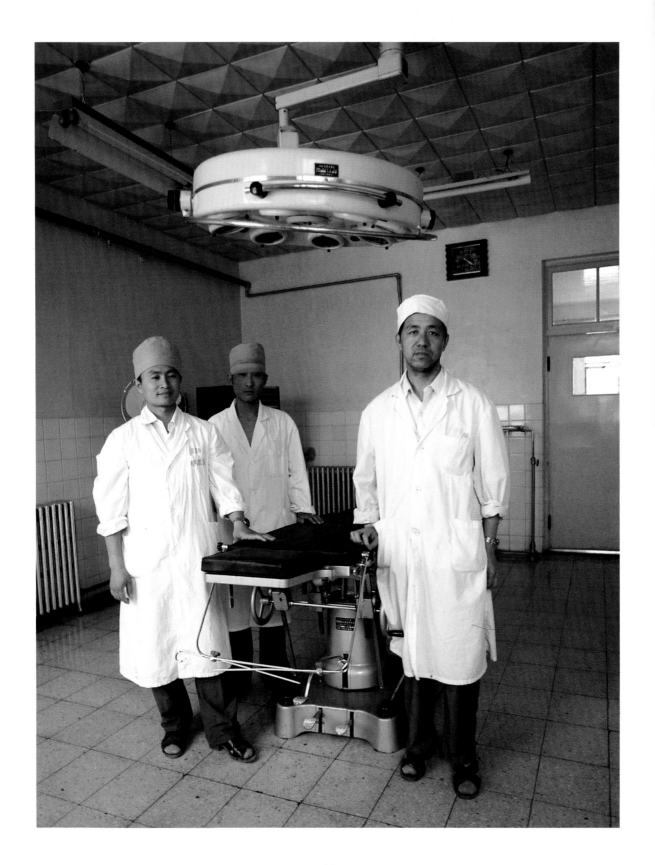

134

The base hospital at the Peking Third Garrison Division has none of the modern amenities associated with a British Forces Hospital. The X-ray equipment was a ten-year-old design. On the other hand, the PLA's doctors were treating their patients with natural medicines and acupuncture, a treatment rarely practised, if at all, in European military hospitals. Here a medical assistant is working in the hospital's sterilization unit.

Tired and exhausted medical staff in their operating room peer blearily at the camera. Judging by the lack of anaesthetic equipment, operations were probably conducted by acupuncture.

save Wang's hands. After the operation Dr Lu Yupu, head of the hospital's Orthopaedic Department, said that Wang would have her hands working again in about two months. What courage that young woman had – for only her arms were anaesthetized during the operation.

Escorted by a growing stream of medical staff, I strolled through the endless hospital corridors, for understandably my hosts were keen to show me everything, from the pharmacy to the birth control centre. Although my knowledge of medicine and hospitals is limited it was apparent that much of the equipment was dated. In spite of this lack of modern equipment in many departments, as a visitor I could not help but be impressed by the quiet professionalism shown by the doctors and medical workers, swathed in white caps and gowns. In one office, doctors were writing up their own notes at plain tables, since the luxury of medical secretaries was non-existent. The operating theatre was bare simplicity, with only one operating table and a large lamp looming down like some giant eye.

Everywhere was spotlessly clean, but the slick regimentation associated with many military hospitals was absent. In the small six-bed wards, patients chatted with their visitors while others read. There were some with private rooms; one of them was a political commissar who had rendered long and faithful service to the Motherland.

We went outside and on into a collection of dilapidated outbuildings which, much to my surprise, turned out to be the hospital's drug bottling unit. Two PLA medical staff were sterilizing and filling small glass ampoules with drugs. Again their equipment was vintage. However, you could not help but admire their determination. They were struggling to be self-sufficient despite the failings of the tools and machinery they had at their disposal. In an adjoining room, the sealed ampoules were labelled and packed into cardboard containers ready for use. The acrid smell from the sterilization process became overpowering.

A gnawing fatigue had plagued me all afternoon and as I was leaving the drug bottling unit, my eyes failed to focus. I found myself dripping with perspiration. I put out a hand to steady myself, when from somewhere I heard Mr Gu saying, 'Are you all right, Mr Young? Do you need a doctor?'

I must have nodded or said something, for I was immediately supported and taken to a nearby room. I felt detached from my body, existing outside it. I sensed that everyone around me was concerned. My blood pressure was taken and I was asked to place a thermometer under my armpit. Somewhere in the background I

China's one-child family policy is as strongly enforced in the PLA as it is in the rest of the country. Such families have their rewards: namely, income subsidies and priority housing. The birth of other children could, on the other hand, bring about economic penalties for a family. Some government officials believe that the effects of this policy will not be realized for another ten years. This specialist on birth control lectures and gives advice to PLA families.

Many Western physicians are sceptical of the benefits of acupuncture. However, this 2,500-year-old form of treatment is widely used by the PLA's doctors, whose patients include the civilian population as well as military personnel. Surprisingly, medical treatment is not free in China; for those who can afford it, a small fee is charged. At this PLA hospital a doctor gives acupuncture treatment to a member of the local community who has sustained head injuries.

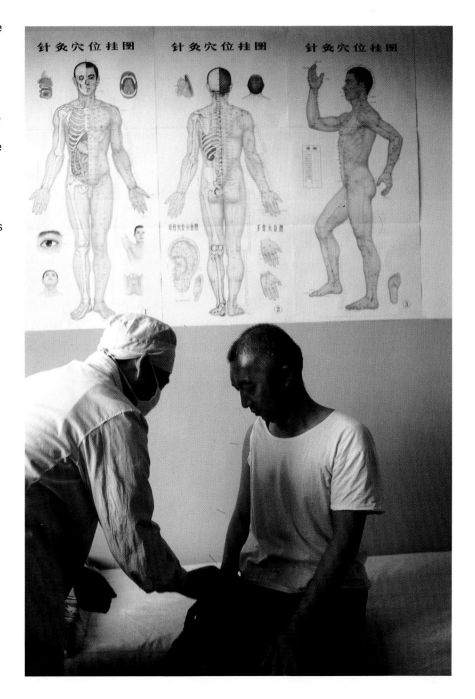

heard the sound of camera shutters. Whatever would they want pictures for, I wondered? Around me people were speaking in soft voices.

Mr Gu translated what the doctor was saying: 'You have a high temperature and a fever, Mr Young. The doctor is going to give you some natural medicines and has asked me to assure you that there will be no after-effects. You are to go to bed at once. He will also prescribe tablets for the dysentery.' They gave me three small packets and Mr Gu explained the dosage. He counted out the tablets; there were about seven in all, which I took with some water. They guided me to the car and within minutes I was in bed in my room, wrapped in blankets and asleep. Looking back, it seems likely that I can claim to be the first Western journalist to be treated in a PLA hospital.

I awoke to find my two minders, Mr Gu and Mr Chen, observing me rather glumly from the foot of the bed. The sound of their entry into the room must have woken me. 'How are you feeling now, Mr Young?' asked Mr Gu.

It took a little time to reply. After collecting my thoughts I replied: 'I'm feeling much better, thank you. Whatever they were, those drugs worked.' Slowly I swung my legs over the side of the bed, paused for a few seconds, then stood up. The dizziness had gone and I was no longer hot and perspiring. I looked out of the window; the sun was now casting long shadows across the corn field from the poplars outside. 'What time is it?' I asked.

Members of the Peking Third Garrison Division enjoy a game of basketball in the cool evening. The tournament attracts a wide audience of both men and women from all sections of the garrison. Although the women are in uniform, several of them decide to wear dainty Western shoes and stockings. Some wear their hair shoulder-length, a style which certainly would not have been tolerated a few years ago.

'Nearly seven o'clock,' Mr Gu replied. I remembered the basketball game and the visit to the barracks which had been planned for the evening. Within three hours the drugs had brought the fever under control and though still weak, at least I could work.

Some days later Mr Gu told me that at the time he had seriously considered taking me back to Peking until I had fully recovered. Being a guest of the PLA, it would have been a grave embarrassment for them if anything serious had happened to me. In China everything is a matter of face.

Mr Chen would not let me carry my camera bag, taking it from me to carry with his own. I snapped a lens onto my Leica R4 and slipped it over my shoulder, making my way down the stairs of the barrack block. We took our time crossing the dusty square; the last of the sunlight cast a warm orange glow around everything. A whistle blew in the distance and figures in red and blue outfits began darting around the basketball court in the soft evening light. The game had begun.

It took over a week for me to recover fully from the effects of the fever. Each evening, Dr Zhang Xiaojin would visit me. Her

139

evening ritual was always the same; she would give me a thermometer to place under my armpit – then for several minutes would look at me, only glancing away to discuss some point or other with Mr Gu my interpreter. At first it was quite unnerving. One evening I asked why she always looked at me so intently. She then explained that Chinese doctors were trained to observe their patients in great detail. Observation was an important part of traditional Chinese medical training. Circumstances had made it necessary for me to place myself in the care of PLA doctors, and of one thing I am certain: without the benefit of their traditional Chinese drugs, my recovery would certainly have been prolonged.

Although the PLA is modernizing, it will always retain certain elements of its guerrilla army heritage. Since the one commodity that China has in abundance is people, the 'People's War' concept is at the very heart of its defence strategy. She will still employ the tactic of enticing the invader into her land, and then at predetermined points, will envelop them within a mass of her fighters. Although this is a traditional Chinese defence technique, it is one

The marching and drill of the PLA retains many of the characteristics of the Soviet Bloc countries. When the troops pass the reviewing stand they have already broken into a strenuous goose-stepping style march.

White-gloved members of the Peking Third Garrison Division display bayonet-fighting techniques. All of them are wearing the newly-designed summer army uniform.

During bayonet practice, PLA fighters shout out battle cries in unison *(inset)*.

which, with modifications, will still be used as a front-line defensive manoeuvre.

The stereotype 'millet and rifle' guerrilla fighter of the Long March era, however, is a thing of the past. He is now being retrained and reorganized into a mechanized army. There are now some select units that have an Armoured Personnel Carrier (APC) tank or truck for every six soldiers. In future only a fifth of the PLA's ground forces will be infantry. The Chinese have learnt that it is essential both to move the foot soldier fast and to develop a combined operations mentality. There is at least one military school in the Nanjing Military Region (MR) which has been brought into being for the sole purpose of this kind of training, and along their Russian border, the Chinese have recently formed one of their latest PLA units; a mechanized Army Corps with combined operations strike ability. It comprises infantry, armour, electronic and anti-chemical warfare contingents, along with anti-aircraft defences and several fighter squadrons. Linking everything is a computer system co-ordinating all operations and firepower, including missiles.

More than anything else, though, I wanted to meet the PLA fighter at close quarters; to see him drilling and observe how he handled his weapons. In order to do this I travelled scores of miles on the narrow farm roads of Shuni and Champing counties to the north-east of Peking. At three different units, all part of the Peking Garrison Division, I met infantry soldiers, tank crews and gunners. They were located in areas well away from any tourist route; on none of my journeys did I meet or see another European. Without my two cadre escorts, and Ministry of Defence approval, I would not have been allowed into these areas. It must be remembered that although China is promoting tourism, and encouraging foreign business, many rural areas are forbidden territory to the visitor.

I was taken to the Eleventh Regiment of the Third Garrison Division in the Peking Military District, as a guest of the Regimental Commander, Mr Wang Wen Kuei. As always on these occasions, an elaborate programme had been arranged – it was never possible to just 'drop in' to watch the day's training. The publicity-minded PLA were constantly aware that they must present themselves in the very best light to this foreign observer.

There could still be further changes in the PLA's newly designed uniforms: refinements to winter dress have still to be made. Although the ranking system within the PLA has been approved, there is little indication of what the ranking insignia may be. This young infantry soldier (left) is armed with the type 56 7.62 mm semi-automatic rifle, which is equipped with a folding spiked bayonet. The sentry above is wearing the summer working dress of the PLA fighter. His empty ammunition pouch is a dated design still being used in the PLA.

China's infantry soldier is regarded by military experts to be one of the world's finest. He is highly motivated and extremely fit, capable of covering long distances on foot, although there are an increasing number of infantry units of the PLA being equipped with fast-moving armoured personnel carriers (APCs).

The Chinese infantry soldier is known to be most effective at close quarters and an increasing amount of his training is being directed towards night operations. This infantry fighter is demonstrating camouflage technique for daylight manoeuvres.

After normal working hours the headquarters of the Peking Third Garrison Division is in the care of the daily Duty Officer whose responsibility it is to inform the Garrison Commander of any emergencies. He sleeps next to his office while on duty.

As military salaries are low, the purchase of a daily newspaper by everyone is rare and something of a luxury. So daily and military newspapers are made available to everyone by way of the local noticeboard.

There was a specially-constructed enclosed viewing stand with air-conditioning, built for visiting heads of state, and it was a pleasant relief to escape into it from the ninety degree heat as I watched a squad of PLA infantry being drilled on the cement square. They performed their marching and drill routine Russian fashion, dressed in ill-fitting lightweight summer uniforms and white cotton gloves. Meanwhile, over on my right, another group stripped and assembled a selection of infantry weapons, which included several machine-guns and mortars.

The Eleventh Regiment has approximately 2,800 officers and men, part of an Infantry division of some thirteen thousand which is supported by specialist units of anti-chemical, flame-throwing and recoilless rifle companies. As I watched these PLA foot soldiers at close quarters, it was only natural that I should draw a comparison between them and certain NATO units I had visited. There was no denying that there was a youthful eagerness in everything these young soldiers did; in military terms, they were highly motivated. But they did not possess that fine military snap seen in a Guards Regiment or the US Marine Corps. Even in civilian clothes, members of these élite units are recognizable. This is not to say that the PLA are not capable of military precision. On the contrary, I have seen PLA guards of honour who were exceptionally well-drilled. I have also seen other units marching eighteen abreast, and breaking into the strenuous goosestep with unerring accuracy as they passed the reviewing stand.

The Chinese have a natural affinity for the martial arts and

There is a distinct Eastern Bloc appearance about the new headwear of the PLA.

a selected group of PLA fighters gave me an impressive demon-stration. Bodies were hurled through the air in a most effective manner, clenched fists unleashed with the ferocity of coiled springs to dispatch an opponent crashing to the ground. I was watching them in practice when their punches were pulled; in combat, to be at the receiving end of any one of these punches would mean instant death.

Specialist PLA units are taught Putu, one of several forms of Chinese martial arts.

The People's Liberation Army Artillery Regiments are – in the opinion of Western experts – well-trained and effective. Even though a great deal of their hardware is of a thirty-year-old design, in the field, together with first class infantry, they present a formidable force. It is this kind of combination that provides a powerful attacking force, ideally suited to mountain and jungle terrain – like the Vietnam border areas, which the Chinese invaded in 1979.

To watch the PLA's gunners handle their equipment I was taken to the Third Division's Artillery Regiment at Nulan Shan in Shunyi County. The strength of the regiment numbered some twelve hundred officers and men. By now it was nearing the height

146

of summer and it was not unusual for the daily temperatures to be in the low nineties. After the customary speeches of welcome I was taken to watch a display of field gun handling. Three groups of gunners were paraded on the square with their guns; these were two ancient-looking, though well maintained, 1950s-style Soviet model howitzers, and a much rarer nineteen-tube mobile rocket launcher. The bulk of the regiment's guns was parked along the edge of the square, which, from the goal posts at each end, obviously doubled as the regimental football pitch.

After watching the usual drills of elevating, turning, and slamming dummy shells into the breech, I asked if I could take some pictures. The manoeuvres were repeated with the same precision and dexterity several times to obtain a detailed coverage. As I was taking my last shots Mr Gu asked me to hurry as the gunner who was loading was burning his hands on the shell! Once again, it was a question of face. To have told me that the shell was too hot would have meant a loss of face for everyone taking part. I asked to be taken to the gunner to express my apologies. Fortunately, his hands had not blistered; when I spoke with him he

Another example of vintage weaponry still being used by the PLA is this thirty-year-old Soviet-designed 122 mm Howitzer field gun. However, it is still a very effective weapon, regardless of its age.

A young PLA conscript, one of a seven-man crew, demonstrates the loading of a Howitzer field gun.

assured me he had no pain. Afterwards, I strolled over to the pile of shells lying in the sun. Placing the palm of my hand on one of them, I drew it away again instantly. The shell was red-hot!

After a hectic drive through the farming areas of Champing County we arrived at Nankou, home of the PLA's Sixth Tank Division. I very much doubt if I shall ever experience such a reception again; several crews, some fifty men in all, dressed in the protective rubber headgear and two piece coveralls worn by Chinese tank crews, gave me a clapping welcome as soon as I stepped out of the car. At the far end of the line was a message of welcome on a schoolroom blackboard, written in large Chinese characters with various coloured chalks.

The People's Liberation Army is well aware that its eleven thousand strong tank force is obsolete. The Soviet-inspired Type 59s and 62s in their original form are very basic armour, easily outgunned in any conflict against their modern Soviet counter-parts. As well as having superior weapons, the Soviets have 41,150 more tanks than the Chinese. Until they can acquire the funds and the technology, therefore, the PLA must improvise – and the West should never underestimate the resourcefulness of the Chinese. To mitigate the deficiencies in their armour, they have retained the chassis of the Type 59s and 62s, modernized them, and provided them with more firepower. The converted Type 59s have subse-quently been redesignated T69.

From Britain they obtained a highly successful gun – the 105 mm L7 – and from other sources they obtained night sights and

Tank crews clapped on my arrival at their Nankou headquarters; on a large blackboard was a message of welcome written in beautiful Chinese characters.

149

The armoured divisions of the PLA are equipped with 11,450 tanks of varying vintage including several thousand Type 59s. British and Israeli technology has assisted the Chinese in making significant improvements to tank weaponry and fire control systems. This four man tank crew parades in front of the Type 59 at their Nankou headquarters.

PLA tank crews wear protective headgear – a protection against head injury which could occur inside the tank when travelling over rough terrain. Seated in a turret cupola, this machine-gunner is equipped with a 12.7 mm Type 54 anti-aircraft machine-gun; belt fed, it has an effective range of 2,000 metres.

As the Chinese economy improves, family savings are being spent on home luxuries: radios, television sets and refrigerators.

Regimental Commander Mr Ma Pei Wei invited me to his home after I had spent some time with his tank regiment.

laser rangefinders, along with a stabilized turret, rubber tracks and a ballistic computer in the fire control system. In addition, the tank regiments are now equipped with a new amphibious light tank which the Chinese have designated the Type 63. They have updated their tank squadrons at a cost their defence budget can afford and, for the time being, the vulnerability of the PLA's armoured divisions has been contained.

In the meantime, the National Defence, Science, Technology and Industry Commission, chaired by Ding Henggao, is known to be experimenting with a tank similar to Britain's Challenger.

After watching a display of gunnery by two of the tank crews on a small electronic firing range, the Regimental Commander, Mr Ma Pei Wei, invited me to his home. His wife and nine-year-old son, dressed in his Young Pioneers uniform, were waiting on the steps of their PLA house. A traditional Chinese welcome had been arranged for all of us – for I was accompanied by eight officers from the regiment as well as my two Peking cadres. There were cold flannels for everyone, soft drinks, sweets in bright crinkly paper and, best of all, large slices of juicy melon.

It was a welcome break to see the inside of a military home, and to gorge slices of cold melon whilst admiring the family's Japanese fridge and watch Ma Zhi Xiao, their small son, twiddle the knobs of their shiny, brand new radio.

This was the China I enjoyed – seeing families in their homes and being invited to participate in a small part of their daily lives.

Regretfully, it was time to go. I took one last drink of orange, the Commander's wife pressed some sweets into my hand, we said our goodbyes and I strolled out to the waiting car. The Regimental Commander led the way in his car to the main gates. Everyone waved as we sped away down the country road leaving a swirling trail of dust.

In the back seat Mr Gu turned to me and said: 'Tomorrow we are with the Air Force – another long day, I'm afraid.'

Nine-year-old Ma Zhi Xiao twiddled controls of the family's recently purchased Japanese radio in the small bedroom.

6 Fighter Pilots of the Thirty-Eighth

The world of flying was one of my youthful preoccupations. During the school summer holidays, in those hot summers of the early forties, which I would invariably spend with my aunt in Norfolk, I would cycle miles, visiting the American air bases which at that time surrounded the small village of Garboldisham.

Equipped with a small vintage brass telescope and from the security of a farmer's hedge or wood, I would watch B17s return to their bases in scattered formations, the local group insignia of a bright yellow triangle on their large rudders. Some would be struggling to maintain height, trailing smoke with one, sometimes two, engines feathered. Their fighter cover would fly low over the woods near to my aunt's cottage – Mustangs and Thunderbolts mostly. I watched them lower their gear on the downwind leg, then make a long descending curve for the final approach.

Years later in Canada, for the sheer fun of it, I obtained a commercial pilot's licence and fulfilled a boyhood dream. At weekends I would fly a small float plane from a quiet lake in Canada's western province of Alberta. Such memories of my youth returned as we once again skirted the centre of Peking, and routed south-east in the direction of Tianjin City on our way to the base of the Thirty-Eighth Division of the PLA Air Force near Yang Cun.

Since its inception on November 11 1949, the People's Liberation Army Air Force has grown to be the third largest in the world, after the United States and the Soviet Union. Back in 1940 it inherited twenty-one airfields and eighty-eight aircraft from the Chinese Nationalist Air Force, when they fled to Taiwan. Now Western intelligence sources list 383 airfields of varying lengths and surfaces. There are in excess of five thousand combat aircraft, crewed and serviced by 490,000 personnel. Of these, 4,500 are fighters and 620 are bombers. In addition, there are an estimated 1,500 training aircraft and four hundred helicopters. However, its size in no way reflects PLAAF's effectiveness in Western air war terms. Flying boats, for example, are still being deployed in a defence role, making China one of the few countries in the world

Some of the fighter pilots of the Thirty-Eighth Division of the People's Liberation Army Air Force. Some are instructors while others are flying China's front line fighter, the F6. Stepping from their crew bus, these pilots immediately put on their g-suits before the group photograph was taken.

still doing so: the BE6 is used in reconnaissance and anti-submarine warfare. The bombers are outmoded Ilyushin 28s and Tupolev 16s.

There are an estimated three thousand F6 fighters in operational service with China's air force, which, certainly numerically, indicates that it is one of their most important front line fighters. Together with the A5 Fantan, a low altitude, high speed fighter bomber, which several Western experts believe was designed to be an all-weather aircraft, the F6 certainly has its origins in the agile Soviet MiG19. As an all-weather aircraft the A5 Fantan was a failure, owing to China's lack of avionics and radar technology. China's air force is known to be operating six hundred of these aircraft, including one hundred that are flying as part of the air-arm of the Navy. Two venerable fighters of the fifties that the Chinese are still flying are MiG15s and 17s, the latter classified as the F5. There are tandem-seater versions of both these aircraft, for use as jet trainers.

It would appear that when China was considering the overall defence policy of the Motherland she instinctively placed her trust in two things: the rapid research and development of her nuclear and missile technology, and the sheer numbers of troops that she had at her disposal, who in time would be re-educated and re-equipped. Adopting such a policy had its dangers. There is little doubt that China's nuclear weaponry has been developed at the expense of her conventional forces and nowhere is this more evident than in her military aircraft design and construction. As it is with the Super Powers, so China's first line of defence is now her nuclear missiles. Although they may lack multiple warheads, they are nevertheless capable of reaching targets several thousand miles away.

So the message from Peking to any would-be aggressor is conclusive: if attacked, a nuclear counter-offensive would be likely. Everyone knows that China's Air Force and Navy pilots are still flying aircraft that were designed well over thirty years ago. Aware of these deficiencies, the National Defence Science, Technology and Industry Commission is busily cutting back on the dated aviation technology they inherited from the Russians. Ever conscious of cost, the Chinese government are tantalizingly offering their military hardware for sale around the world in a supreme effort to obtain the necessary finance for development of its own weapons. Understandably, there is growing concern by a number of Western nations on learning that China has recently supplied Iran with two hundred HY2 Silkworm anti-ship missiles.

When the Soviets withdrew their technical aid to the Chinese between 1959 and 1960 it had a disastrous effect on China's military aircraft construction. Overnight, China's aeronautical 'apprenticeship' had been severed, leaving her aircraft technicians in an aviation backwater for the better part of a decade. Another crucial deficiency in China's air power lies in her pilot training programme: flying times for front line operational pilots are low, while there is little evidence that pilots are trained in advanced flying techniques such as contour flying and in-flight refuelling.

As far as in-flight refuelling and training for this complex operation is concerned, this could change in the near future. A British company has recently carried out a design study for the China Air Force regarding the feasibility of the A5 Fantan being adapted for this purpose; this would also involve modifications to the Tupolev 16 bomber which would act as the tanker aircraft.

There is little doubt that China's most advanced fighter is the F8; a plus Mach two, twin-engined, delta-winged, high altitude fighter-interceptor, which is a Chinese-produced version of the Soviet MiG21 series. The cockpit configuration of the F8 will most certainly be based on sixties' technology. However, this aircraft is in the process of receiving a technical facelift from a five hundred million dollar avionics package from the United States. When the conversion is complete the F8 will have an all-weather, day-night operational performance. China is reported to have some fifty F8s in operation and, while the conversion programme could take up to six years to complete, it is believed that there are modified F8s already in front line service. For some time now there has been unconfirmed speculation concerning a swing-winged fighter powered by Rolls-Royce Spey engines with the designation of F12. So far the F12 remains no more than speculative military rumour.

Despite the comments from some quarters that the F8 when modified will be no more than an advanced obsolete aircraft, its presence in China's airspace is causing grave concern. There is an uneasiness both from within the United States government, as well as from several Asian countries, concerning the superiority that the People's Republic of China will have in the air, once all its F8s are fitted with new technology. Whilst the updated F8s are no match against current Soviet fighters, they are certainly superior to anything that China's non-Communist neighbours are flying – including Taiwan. China's air superiority could have far reaching consequences throughout the whole of Asia, especially over the Taiwan Strait.

The PLA's air transport fleet is considered by Western analysts

There are an estimated 1,500 training aircraft being used by the People's Liberation Army Air Force. Some trainee pilots are flying cleverly-converted MiG17s which the Chinese designated the F5, while other student pilots are flying two seater MiG15s and Yak 18As. Compared to NATO air forces, pilot training hours are low. So, until Chinese military aircraft are equipped with better technology, and pilot training is improved, the scope for all-weather operations by the Air Force is certainly limited.

as being 'poor to fair'. They appear to have approximately 550 transports, made up of various types of Ilyushin and Anatov. The Chinese are known to have thirty British Aerospace Tridents along with ten BA 146s; of these, eight Tridents are reported to be on military service. Obviously to offset running costs, the PLA is utilizing some of its transport aircraft in a civilian role, hoping to improve the efficiency of the national airline, China Airways. Aircraft inherited from the Nationalists, the forty-year-old C46 'Commandos', are still believed to be flown by the PLAAF.

To update her ageing air force, China would like to obtain the Lockheed C130 Hercules, as well as the British Aerospace Harrier vertical short take-off and landing close support fighter. When I spoke of the Harrier to Chinese Air Force officers, they all agreed that it was an aircraft they would like to procure, but they complained of its high cost and British unwillingness to negotiate a competitive production deal!

We drove southwards through the lush countryside of Hebei Province, with its narrow rural roads and inevitable long avenues

157

of poplars. Many stretches of the road were deserted and it was difficult to think of Hebei as having a population of fifty-one million people. Here in the countryside the dialect of the peasant, with its more pronounced burr, is clearly more of the soil than that spoken by the commissars of Peking. Cotton is one of the main crops for the local farmers, along with wheat, maize, millet and tobacco. Everywhere China's new spirit of private enterprise could be seen – farm workers were busy in the fields, while in the villages we passed through, everyone appeared to be buying or selling something, from chickens to vegetables and eggs.

Apparently, the airfield was difficult to find, since on more than one occasion our driver turned the car round after asking the way from passing cyclists, and made back in the direction we had just come. As often as not, military airfields around the world are tucked away in difficult-to-find places, and the PLAAF Thirty-Eighth Fighter Division at Yan Cun was no exception. Leaving the firm rural road, we turned on to what appeared to be a farm access, crossed a single track railway, and then found ourselves within the airfield. I knew we had arrived as soon as a sleepy-looking guard stepped out

Married quarters for the pilots of the Thirty-Eighth Fighter Division and their families are modest: the accommodation on the base was brick-built and arranged in long dreary lines. All were growing some variety of vegetable in their small gardens. A communal pathway led to each house, all of the same size, comprising a living room, kitchen, dining room and bedroom. Kitchens were basic: mostly containing only a stove and a selection of kitchen utensils. Floors were concrete and uncovered.

into the middle of the road and waved us on with his AK47.

We passed well-concealed aircraft bunkers, among which ground personnel were manoeuvring aircraft on a concrete turning area. The road widened into a large taxiway, where a line of dilapidated weather-beaten F6 fighters were parked, minus their Red Star national markings. Further along were two aircraft which would have delighted any aircraft 'spotter': the Antonov AN2 (Colt), which the Chinese call the Fong Show, and the BT6, an adaptation of the Soviet YAK 18. Looking around at the outbuildings as I stepped from the car, I was reminded of the derelict Second World War airfields, still seen in odd corners of the British countryside.

By now, I was becoming familiar with the arrival procedure at the units I had been cleared to visit. Cold flannels, cold drinks – orange or beer – and consideration of my requirements. Once everyone had settled down and grown accustomed to each other, I would be able to make notes and ask questions through my interpreter. After being warned about how sensitive some officers might be about tape recorders, I avoided using one. Instead, I

For those who could afford them, luxuries would include a fan, refrigerator and a radio or television. Most service families appeared to be able to afford most of these items. Squadron Leader Chi Bing Quan, who has been flying for ten years, is pictured sitting proudly with his wife Gong Xiao Mei and their five-year-old daughter Chi Fang Fang.

159

would make as many notes as time would allow, observe, then in the evening write up my diary.

I liked the Deputy Commander of the Thirty-Eighth within a few minutes of meeting him. Mr Shen Xue Li had a kind face, and his eyes had the faraway look of a man who had spent many hours scanning wide skies and distant horizons. He later told me that he had been flying for thirty-two years. He wore the lightweight summer dress uniform, Soviet-style hat, open-necked white shirt outside a pair of dark blue trousers. The only differences from his army counterparts were the blue patches on his collar, and the blue band around the hat.

During my time with the PLAAF, I received a great deal of help from Mr Shen Xue Li. He would point out the best angles from which to photograph the aircraft, and – with the exception of allowing me to look into cockpit interiors – he gave me total access to his aircraft and pilots.

Much to my disappointment, however, it was not possible for me to be accommodated on the airbase. Instead, arrangements had been made for me to sleep at the PLA barracks no more than ten minutes' drive away.

It transpired that the flying programme depended very much on the weather – which I thought was overly cautious even for student pilots, let alone a front line combat squadron. The local report was for scattered thunderstorms; however, there was a ten thousand feet cloud base in the local area and near unlimited visibility. It was a lovely evening for flying, with the wind at less than five knots. Already there was a pinkness in the sky as the sun began to slip behind the horizon. Quite a contrast to the adverse weather conditions in which I had witnessed Sea Harrier and Sea King pilots flying from the Royal Navy's *Ark Royal* a few weeks earlier.

Western experts agree that China's Air Force is genuinely limited to fairweather flying operations, because most of its aircraft lack all-weather radar instrumentation and ground control, and it follows that without all-weather strike technology, their pilots inevitably lack certain types of flying experience which would enable them to strike a target in minimal conditions. The Chinese are negotiating with several Western countries in an effort to acquire the technology and pilot training to overcome these deficiencies, but as senior government officials told me: 'It must be at the right price, and with no political strings attached.' The Chinese are natural, shrewd businessmen: whenever possible they will only purchase hardware which involves producing equipment in China under licence.

Ground crews at the Yan Cun Air Force base manoeuvre aircraft around the dispersal area.

Student Air Force pilots do their basic training on Chinese modified YAK 11s and 18s. They are selected from Senior Stage Middle School students, and from the age of eighteen may apply for aptitude training. Pilot training is a three-year programme, followed by a further three years with an operational unit. Senior air force officers told me that there was a twenty per cent failure rate, but I suspect this was a conservative estimate. Annual flying hours appeared to be low in comparison with the NATO air forces. One of their flight instructors, a squadron leader, told me that he had only logged 1,400 flying hours after ten years' flying. Some of the other pilots I spoke with averaged less than ten flying hours a month.

Inside the small two-storey control tower, the aircraft controller chattered intently on the radio. One of the instructors came down the stairs and gave an informal flight briefing on the evening's sortie to the group of waiting pilots. Deputy Commander Shen Xue Li beckoned me over and informed me through my interpreter that, although bad weather was predicted, the evening's flying would not be affected.

Instead of the pilots being taken by transport, or making their

Maintenance crews service
an F6 in a hangar at the Yang
Cun fighter base near Tianjin.

way independently to their aircraft, there was a squadron ritual. Marching two abreast, the pilots paraded to their waiting jets. The ground crews stood in line and saluted them. Then, while one of the pilots completed the external checks, the other was assisted into the cockpit and strapped in by one of the technicians. Surprisingly, none of the pilots was wearing a g-suit.

There appeared to be no shortage of ground crew: dressed in dark blue coveralls and large straw hats, three men were assigned to each aircraft for the pre-take-off preparations. On one occasion, I saw more than a dozen ground crew move one F6 fighter around the tarmac. In any of the NATO air forces, no more than three ground crew would have been needed to move the same size aircraft – one hauling the machine by tractor, and a man on each wingtip. When I remarked on this to one of the officers, he smiled and said: 'There is one thing we have plenty of in China – people!'

Once the external checks were complete, the young fliers lost no time in firing up their engines and taxiing out to the single hard runway which ran in a north-westerly/south-easterly direction. With the minimum of delay as soon as the jets reached the end of the taxiway they made a sweeping left turn onto the runway centre line, slowly fed in the power and commenced their take-off roll. The jets crackled in the still evening air as in quick succession they took off. Within minutes it was silent again and all that remained was the pungent smell of jet fumes.

Within the hour all had returned. Before landing they flew over the field at two thousand feet and made a wide left-hand circuit, before lining up for their approach. By the time the last one had landed, I was enjoying a light meal of rice and tomatoes in my room. In the last light of day, I could see the change in the weather that had been forecast; the first low clouds began to roll in, and the thunderstorms continued until dawn.

As I expected there was no flying the following day, even though the poor overnight weather conditions had begun to improve.

It was my sheer good fortune that on the day I returned to the Thirty-Eighth for further flying pictures, there, on the runway, being refuelled, was their low altitude, high speed fighter bomber, the A5 Fantan. There were two aircraft, both painted white, indicating they could be attached to the PLA's Naval Air Arm which has some eight hundred aircraft of various types. The two A5s were at Yang Cun for an afternoon's bombing practice and there were no objections to photography. Analysts regard it as a fair-weather aircraft with an estimated Mach 1.5 performance.

China is divided into seven military air regions, with Air Force Headquarters located in Peking. The A5 pictured overleaf, known by its NATO codename as the Fantan, is a low-altitude high-speed fighter bomber, which has certain MiG19 characteristics. The Air Force is known to be operating six hundred of these aircraft, a hundred of which are being flown by the Navy's air arm.

Improvements have been made on the aircraft in recent years; the A5 may be one of the first in the Chinese Air Force capable of being refuelled in flight from a Tupolev 16 bomber, acting as the tanker aircraft.

A PLA pilot takes a break during a practice bombing exercise to confer with his squadron commander. He is dressed only in a casual summer uniform and it is interesting to note that he is flying without a g-suit, limiting his performance in being able to take the aircraft through high-speed manoeuvres.

There are two versions of the aircraft; one housing a radar in the nose, the other without. The A5 without radar is easily recognizable by its nose pitot boom and the three IFF aerials underneath.

Like most of the flyers I had seen with the Thirty-Eighth, these A5 pilots were not wearing g-suits, which limited their ability to perform manoeuvres such as high speed turns. Their flying clothing was simple: white flying helmet (bonedome) and a lightweight khaki blouse over loose-fitting dark blue trousers.

One of the pilots sauntered out to his refuelled A5; no sooner had he settled into the cockpit than he fired up his two engines, each giving 7,165 lbs of static thrust. His cockpit checks complete, he began to taxi, at the same time lowering the upward hinged canopy. The holding point was less than two hundred metres away. He was airborne within three minutes; the two pin-points of light – flames from the engines – growing smaller by the second.

I was hoping to see a low scorching bombing run across the field to the target area at the far end, but I was to be disappointed. Instead, the A5 pilot approached the target in a shallow dive starting from ten thousand feet; he levelled off at a thousand feet, released the practice bomb, then turned away in a left-hand

A young pilot preparing to depart for a practice bombing exercise.

167

climbing turn.

We parked the car on one of the disused runway intersections to observe the landing. It was one of those blistering windless days, the air was thin from the heat, a day when images shimmer on the horizon. With its characteristic nose-high attitude the A5 touched the runway, its undercarriage giving the customary screech. Within seconds of the aircraft's wheels making contact, there was a sharp *thwap* as the pilot released the drag chute. Weaving from side to side, the billowing canopy contributed to the flowing elegance of the A5 as it streaked on down the runway at a hundred miles an hour.

There are women pilots flying with the PLAAF but just how many the Chinese were unwilling to say: I would estimate several hundred. The officers were quick to point out, just as they were in the Army, that women were not trained in combat roles, and emphasized that they only flew transport aircraft. However, I have little doubt that the Chinese women I met would have no trouble flying a jet fighter after a conversion course and weapons systems training.

No one was willing to say how many women pilots were operating in the PLAAF. Some of the young female pilots at the Shahe Air Force Base who were in the final stages of their training on twin-engine aircraft, spoke about their love of flying and the hope of gaining honours for the women of China.

Anxious to meet them, I went out to the Shahe Air Force Base, an hour and a half's drive to the north of Peking, where seven of them, all military pilots with the People's Liberation Army Air Force Transport Command, had agreed to meet me. They all arrived on their shiny new bicycles, dressed in a variety of candy-coloured blouses, revealing dainty Western-style bras beneath. For comfort, they wore their dark blue service trousers, carrying skirts and service dress over the handlebars.

Their feminine dress was a sign of the times among China's young people and part of a much quieter revolution than that of a few years ago. These young women had little in common with the Red Guards of the Cultural Revolution. All were in their early twenties, had mischievous smiles and laughed quietly among themselves as we all shook hands. Then we strolled over to the vintage Ilyushin 14 parked in a nearby dispersal area.

It was cooler under the aircraft. As we spread ourselves under the port wing, the women insisted that I sat on their leather flying jackets, then for the next half hour or so, with Mr Gu's help, we talked flying. It was all the 'in' chatter of any group with a common interest. I was anxious to hear about their training and what the old Ilyushin 14 was like to fly. After selection, the women did their basic training on Yakovlev 18s known as 'Max' by NATO Forces. This aircraft has been modified by the Chinese, and now has squared-off wingtips and rudder and is designated the BT6.

Liu Huafeng, who was not as shy as her six companions, told

China regards each one of her citizens as a potential fighter for the Motherland, and sees her women fighters playing an increasingly dominant role in the country's defence. For some years now the PLAAF has been training young women as pilots to fly their transport aircraft. Most of them appear to fly ancient Ilyushin 14s, carrying cargo to the remote regions of their country. Even though their basic training is identical to that of their male counterparts, senior Air Force officers were quick to deny that women would be trained to fly combat missions.

Liu Huafeng signals the
ground crew before take-off.

me that they had been flying for three and a half years, and were
just completing their night flying training on the IL14. They were
longing to join an operational unit now that their training was
nearly finished. None of them had more than four hundred flying
hours, a third of which were night hours. By now, I expect all will
be flying passengers and cargo in and out of remote airstrips in
some part of China. They were coy about their social lives; one or
two admitted to having pilot boyfriends – but nothing serious.
There seemed to be little chance of a light-hearted love affair. The
Chinese forces discourage any form of fraternization between its
men and women, other than for marriage. When I asked them what
it was they enjoyed most about flying their reply indicated to me
that they had previously been briefed by some political commissar:
'To win honours for the women pilots of China.'

They all saluted smartly one by one as we said our goodbyes.
Tinkling their cycle bells they chanted: 'Please come back and see
us.' Liu was the last to depart as I had been taking photographs of
her. As she slowly cycled away she turned round, waved and
smiled intimately.

In the early hours of the morning Mr Gu and I caught the night
train to Qingdao. It was time to join the Navy.

7 The Sailors of the North Sea Fleet

Every so often, at times in the most unlikely places, you stumble across remnants of China's colonial past. Tianjin railway station is like that.

The British and French established themselves in Tianjin in the middle of the nineteenth century. Following a confrontation with the Chinese, with what has become known as 'Gunboat Diplomacy', the Treaty of Tianjin was signed in 1858, opening the gates for Western countries to trade – especially in opium. Austrians, Germans, Russians, Japanese and Italians were all eager to gain a trading foothold along the Chinese coast. By the early part of the twentieth century, Tianjin was an international settlement. As the Treaty Ports and concessions expanded, each country brought with it its own culture, providing schools, hospitals, police and military establishments.

Even at one o'clock in the morning, the waiting room of Tianjin railway station was an elegant reminder of yesteryear. It was colonial clubland, from the square plaster ceiling with its large six-balled chandelier, down to the potted palm plants and wicker chairs. As I dozed in one of the chairs beside the potted palm, I saw shadows of the past: gents in white crumpled suits, their ladies in cloche hats and white parasols trimmed with lace; rickshaw boys and coolies carrying leather Gladstone bags from the capitals of Europe.

Apart from the odd railway night worker, the station was deserted. Mr Gu and I appeared to be the only passengers joining the night train to Qingdao. One of the officers from the local PLA contingent had accompanied us. Together with the driver of our car, he would locate our reserved soft class compartment, and help load our bags and equipment.

Trains in China have a reputation for being on time and tonight was no exception. As the train approached along the curving platform it was preceded by a shimmering beam of light from the powerful lamp mounted at the front of the engine. It made melodic sounds of hissing steam and clanking pistons. There was a ruddy

At any one time there are 1,800 students at the Academy, as well as an academic staff of several hundred who are housed in campus accommodation. This instructor, like many of the parents on the campus, has found a simple solution for transporting his son to and from school.

glow from the driver's cab and the scraping of a shovel on coal, memorable sounds long gone from Europe's railways.

Train travel in China is a journey into a never-never land of experiences. Even in this so-called egalitarian society, there are four classes of accommodation on trains: soft and hard sleepers and soft and hard seats. Foreigners are expected to travel soft sleeper and it is doubtful if any other ticket would be sold to a visitor. Soft sleeper has four bunks, two on either side. Within a few minutes I was between the sheets of the top bunk nearest the engine. Lulled by the rhythmic sound of wheels on rails, coupled with the gentle swaying of the train, I was soon oblivious to everything around me.

Through the night we thundered across China's northern plain making our way south-east on our 250 mile journey to Qingdao, passing over the Yellow River as dawn was breaking. It was the sound of colliding carriages rippling through the train that finally awakened me. Perhaps something had hit us, I thought. During the night we had been joined by two travelling companions, both Americans; one was of Chinese extraction and the other I was to discover later was California-born and bred. They were salesmen, selling Chinese produce into the markets of West Coast America. 'Casey, do you want some milk?' said the Chinese-American to his companion. Casey sniffled, blew his nose and groaned. All Casey wanted was to rid himself of a cold. He blew his nose again, rolled over on his bunk and went to sleep. I went to the restaurant car for breakfast. Mr Gu declined to join me. He had brought some bread and eggs with him, and sat back in the corner of his bunk, peeled the shell from an egg and continued reading his book.

Soft sleeper accommodation on China's railways has an air of Victorian graciousness; there's a touch of the *Brighton Belle* about everything. The compartments are wood-panelled with lace window curtains, dainty covers, plush seating and table lamps. Large thermos flasks are supplied and replenished at frequent intervals for the traditional *ch'a*. Unfortunately each compartment is linked with a loudspeaker which pours forth endless music and news bulletins as well as travel information. I was told that somewhere on the train was a disc jockey in her own mini studio. However, much to my relief, the soft sleeper class had a volume control on its speaker – unlike other parts of the train which had none! The restaurant car had a similar grandeur to that of the compartment; white table cloths, cutlery, and waitress service. I was late, so there were few people still having breakfast. In broken English the young waitress enquired: 'Eggs fried over – coffee – toasta?' I nodded and thanked her. My appetite was returning after

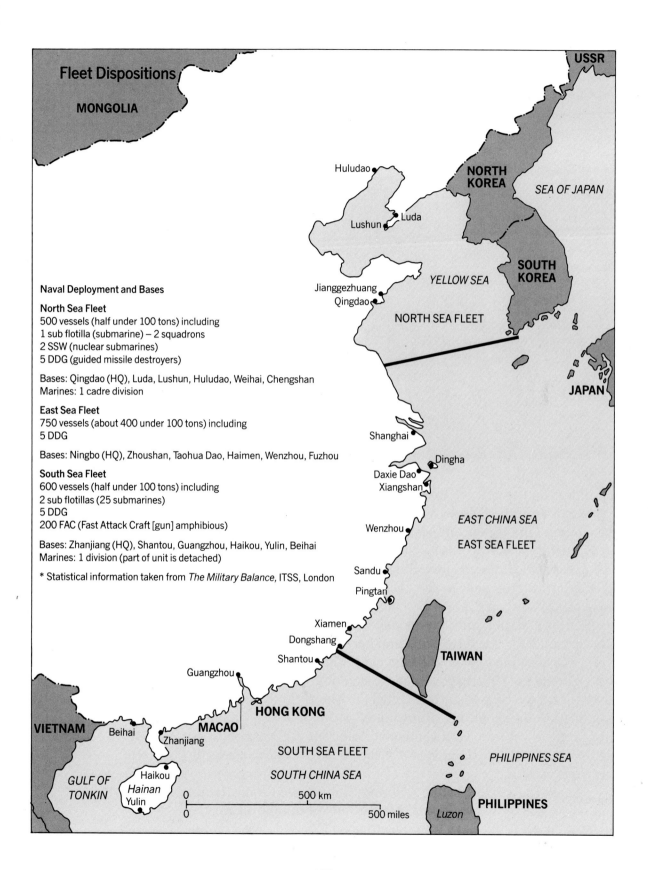

Fleet Dispositions

MONGOLIA

USSR

Huludao

NORTH KOREA

SEA OF JAPAN

Lushun · Luda

SOUTH KOREA

Jianggezhuang

Qingdao

YELLOW SEA

NORTH SEA FLEET

JAPAN

Naval Deployment and Bases

North Sea Fleet
500 vessels (half under 100 tons) including
1 sub flotilla (submarine) – 2 squadrons
2 SSW (nuclear submarines)
5 DDG (guided missile destroyers)

Bases: Qingdao (HQ), Luda, Lushun, Huludao, Weihai, Chengshan
Marines: 1 cadre division

East Sea Fleet
750 vessels (about 400 under 100 tons) including
5 DDG

Bases: Ningbo (HQ), Zhoushan, Taohua Dao, Haimen, Wenzhou, Fuzhou

South Sea Fleet
600 vessels (half under 100 tons) including
2 sub flotillas (25 submarines)
5 DDG
200 FAC (Fast Attack Craft [gun] amphibious)

Bases: Zhanjiang (HQ), Shantou, Guangzhou, Haikou, Yulin, Beihai
Marines: 1 division (part of unit is detached)

* Statistical information taken from *The Military Balance,* ITSS, London

Shanghai

Dingha

Daxie Dao
Xiangshan

Wenzhou

EAST CHINA SEA

EAST SEA FLEET

Sandu

Pingtan

Xiamen

Dongshang

Shantou

Guangzhou

TAIWAN

VIETNAM

Beihai

MACAO

HONG KONG

Zhanjiang

SOUTH SEA FLEET

PHILIPPINES SEA

GULF OF TONKIN

Haikou

Hainan

Yulin

SOUTH CHINA SEA

0   500 km

0   500 miles

Luzon

PHILIPPINES

my illness and almost anything would have been acceptable.

When I returned, Casey was sitting up, wistfully gazing out of the window, and for the umpteenth time that morning, blowing his nose. He did his best to raise a cheery 'Hi', and introduced himself as do all Americans when travelling. Casey was excellent company in spite of his cold and, as the compartment was now empty, we exchanged views on China.

For the first time since my arrival, I was able to escape from my official isolation, converse with another Westerner and, further- more, ask questions. Even with his cold, Casey was amusing. On the Chinese he remarked: 'I have never met such a bunch of capitalists. Each time I return to China the Mercedes that meets me gets bigger!' He shook his pillows and continued: 'And another thing. I have yet to meet a Chinaman who doesn't know how to hustle a buck.' I felt there was a measure of Yankee wisdom in Casey's words.

We arrived at Qingdao at 1.35 pm. The journey from Tianjin had taken exactly twelve hours. Mr Gu looked up and down the platform to see if the Navy were meeting us. I passed Casey on the

Qingdao, a naval and industrial town lying on the coast mid-way between Peking and Shanghai, has always had a European character about it. In 1898 Germany acquired a ninety-nine year lease on Qingdao with the right to build the Shandong railways and to develop the mines. Throughout South-East Asia the town is renowned for its beer, an industry it no doubt inherited from the Germans. Qingdao today is a colourful resort, the playground of high-ranking naval officers and cadres.

platform, surrounded by a dozen or more local business people. One of them was taking his picture. Casey looked exceedingly American in his lightweight suit, and his tie slightly loosened at the collar. We were to meet again a few days later in the departure lounge of Qingdao airport. I was at the bar trying to find enough small change to buy a cold drink, when he came up from behind, slapping me on the back. 'Hiya, John – large world, small place. Let me get that drink for you.' Casey was fully recovered from his cold and longing to be home. Within a few minutes we would be going our separate ways – he to Hong Kong and then to Los Angeles, and I across the Bo Hai Gulf to Dalian on the toe of the Liaodong Peninsula.

PLA naval doctors have a group picture taken by one of their comrades against the background of Qingdao's pier.

It is estimated that there are 360,000 officers and sailors in China's Navy, numerically the smallest of China's armed services.

Women members of the three armed services are allowed to wear stylish blouses beneath their tunics; otherwise their uniforms are similar to those of their male colleagues.

Navy personnel serve for a minimum period of four years. Politically, the Navy is poorly served in Peking's power echelons, with only four representatives looking after their interests, one in the Politburo and three in the Party's Central Committee. What is surprising is that there appears to be no one representing the Navy on the Council of the Ministry of National Defence.

China has a wide-ranging number of vessels but is light on individual ship tonnage. Among her vessels are fast patrol boats, landing craft, frigates, destroyers and submarines. There are even small flotillas of armed junks operated by the People's Militia. Like other branches of the PLA, the Navy suffers from obsolete equipment. At the moment it is primarily a coastal defence force – but there is every indication that this is changing. The Navy is straining to achieve deep-water capabilities and aims to modernize as soon as the money can be found to do so.

One of the Navy's current projects is a new four thousand ton displacement destroyer which will be faster (32–5 knots) and better armed than the present LUDA class. This new deep water vessel will have a longer range and will widen China's defence net. It is being constructed at the Wuhan shipyards and the Chinese, knowing their weaknesses, are incorporating American and French technology into this latest class of destroyer. The power plant is expected to be General Electric 29,000 HP engines, purchased from the United States during the last couple of years, supported by another two diesel engines. The main weapon of this new warship will be a surface-to-surface missile with a performance not unlike that of the French Exocet, supported by 100 mm automatic guns. There will be space for at least two helicopters possibly French Aérospatiale Dauphine Model IIs.

China's Navy is divided into three fleets. The North Sea Fleet is based at Qingdao, with some five hundred ships, protecting the Yellow Sea and the Bo Hai Gulf. The East Sea Fleet, with an estimated 750 vessels, watches over the politically contentious Taiwan Strait. Then there is the South Sea Fleet with another six hundred ships guarding the seas around Hainan Island and the Guangdong coastline. There is also a Naval Air Arm of about eight hundred shore-based aircraft mainly F4s and F6s which includes approximately one hundred A5 Fantan fighter bombers. It is also reported that some 130 Ilyushin 28 torpedo-carrying bombers are available to the Navy.

Thank goodness we were met in Qingdao as we needed help to carry all the equipment! The ever-present Mr Chen had returned to Peking to assemble the historical material I had ordered from his

department. Our car was a magnificent black *Shanghai*, with chrome fittings inside and out. These cars reek with mid-forties elegance and nostalgia, an unforgettable era of yesterday's film heroes: Cagney, Bogart and Edward G. Robinson. Once everything was packed into the vast boot, we roared away from the station with a lusty blare of the horn. I sat on turquoise-coloured seats and peered out at the teeming streets of Qingdao through black net curtains strung across each window. As the driver clunked his way through the gears with an ancient gear shift, Mr Gu chatted to Mr Xia, the naval officer who had just met us.

All the rooms at the front of the hotel where I was staying had views across the Yellow Sea. So, from the balcony of my eighth-floor room, I was able to look out over the red-tiled roofs to a bustling coastline spread out on either side of me. Out in the bay, only a few hundred yards from the shore, an oil drilling platform operated around the clock.

Qingdao is both a naval town and an industrial centre. As well as the headquarters of the North Sea Fleet, it is also a major submarine base with a large submariners' training school. This

Baseball is a popular sport with the young naval students.

seaside resort with its sweeping beaches and white powdery sand is the playground of the cadres, but, as in Portsmouth and Plymouth, the Navy is everywhere.

It is not possible to turn your back on the industrial pollution of Qingdao, with its million and a half inhabitants busily engaged in producing cameras, television sets and watches. They also produce the finest beer in the whole of South-East Asia – a legacy of the city's German past.

I was completely unsure of what to expect from my visit to Qingdao. In Peking there had been grave doubts as to whether or not I would be allowed on board a PLA ship and I had little prospect of being permitted to photograph PLA vessels. Fortunately, and much to my surprise, in Qingdao attitudes changed; the Navy opened its doors to me. It was all due to Mr Xia, the naval officer who had been detailed to look after me during my stay with the North Sea Fleet. The North Koreans, to a lesser extent, also contributed to my good fortune for, had a high-ranking delegation not been visiting Qingdao at the time, the one ship that I was finally permitted to board would not have been in port.

Mr Xia was small in stature, friendly, and had a constant smile – the perfect public relations officer. Through my interpreter Mr Gu, he patiently listened to my needs, from time to time making notes on a small pad. As he left my hotel room, he assured me he would pass on my wishes to his leaders. It would take a little time, but by the following day he should have an answer for me. I was not to be disappointed.

Mr Xia was obviously pleased when we met the following afternoon. Everything that I had requested had been approved. I was told that in my case the Navy had granted an exceptional dispensation and were allowing me on board one of their ships, the J121, a naval survey ship, and I was to be a guest of the Captain and crew the following day.

As soon as the PLA guard at the Qingdao dock gates saw the naval officer inside the *Shanghai*, he waved us through, paying no apparent attention to the Westerner behind its black net curtains. There was a variety of naval craft in port as well as small-tonnage merchant vessels. Tied up, two- and three-deep in one of the basins, were numerous landing craft; further along the quay lay several Hainan class patrol boats and Riga class frigates.

The twelve thousand ton J121 naval survey ship was tied up between a frigate at her bows and several P6 torpedo boats beside her stern; in the far distance I could just make out the outlines of the North Sea Fleet submarine squadrons. We made our way on board along the narrow wood gangway guarded by two smartly-dressed sailors in white summer dress, armed with folding stock AK47s. On board, the ship's company was drawn up in three ranks, their sparkling white tunics and dark blue trousers providing a splash of colour against the monotonous steel grey of the ship.

Unlike his Western counterpart, the Captain in China's Navy is not in sole command of his ship: a PLAN vessel is under the command of two officers: the Captain and the Political Commissar. A dual command structure such as this is bound to produce problems and conflicts. It is not inconceivable that a situation could arise at sea where the authority of the Political Commissar could prevail over the Captain, one of the ways the Party machinery maintains control over the military. Nautical strategy and seamanship may be the responsibility of the Captain, but political strategy, ideology and security is the realm of the Commissar.

As the Captain and the Commissar were not on board that morning, it was the Deputy Captain, Mr Jiang Nan, who took the ship's parade. He was just about to complete his inspection of the ship's company when we arrived. Mr Jiang walked over and joined

The guard at the top of the gangway of the J121 was smartly turned-out in his new lightweight summer uniform and armed with a brand new assault rifle based on the familiar Kalashnikov.

The crew of the J121 return to their ship after a short break in nearby Qingdao.

Deputy Captain Mr Jiang Nan takes the morning parade on the J121. In the background are some of the Navy's submarine berths.

Before parading on the after-deck of the J121, Deputy Captain Mr Jiang Nan inspects his crew.

us, snapping a smart salute as he did so. As we all shook hands he welcomed us aboard the J121 on behalf of the Captain, who had invited us to join him for lunch later.

Clearly the whole ship's company had been detailed to stay on board to welcome the 'round-eyed' visitor. Throughout the ship, sailors were busily engaged in all the routine port duties. Decks were being swilled down, equipment and machinery serviced and uniforms pressed and repaired. As the helicopter hangar was empty, a group of sailors were watching their comrades slice away at a table tennis ball. On the helipad, further up the deck, a louder, more raucous group was pulling and puffing in a gruelling tug-of-war match. Even the Deputy Captain played his part, demonstrating agility with a selection of lifting weights. I was fully aware that everything had been arranged and was a little contrived; nevertheless, there was a genuine desire by everyone to be helpful and make my visit to the ship a success. I had come to Qingdao with few expectations; now I had secured the first pictures ever to reveal something of life on board a Chinese Navy vessel. My stay was not without its restrictions: when I asked if I could photograph some of

Below decks, crew members repair clothing in the officers' quarters of the J121.

The helicopter landing area is located on the after-deck of the J121, with hangar space to accommodate two helicopters. It is also used as a recreational area by the crew; during my visit there were several tug-of-war matches and Mr Jiang Nan, the Deputy Captain, demonstrated his abilities with weights.

the other Navy ships in the harbour, the answer was a firm 'No'!

The long dining table, with its crisp slip-over white cloth, trimmed with red piping, occupied most of what the Royal Navy would call the Ward Room. I counted eighteen chairs around the table, not including the two end places. Each had white slip-over covers, with edge trimming identical to the tablecloth. Only five of us sat down to lunch at this vast table. Captain Wu sat opposite me, between the Political Commissar, Mr Ji Miguei, and the Deputy Captain. The Captain had a kindly face, though he lacked a sense of humour and appeared to be more contemplative than other seafarers I had met over the years. He was dressed in his best cream-coloured tunic, with blue patches and a gold star on each collar. Throughout lunch he listened to Mr Gu who, no doubt, told him of some of the problems he had encountered with this troublesome Western journalist! From time to time he would ask about my home and family along with my impressions of China. It appeared that his home was not far from Qingdao, where he had a wife and two children, a boy and a girl. With the current emphasis in China on one-child families, I wondered what penalties he

Five of us sat down at the twenty-place table in the officers' dining area. Captain Wu (centre) was my host and on his left sat Mr J. Miguei, the political commissar, and on the other side Mr Jiang Nan, the Deputy Captain. My request for this after-lunch photograph came as a total surprise; the table was quickly tidied and the artificial flowers repositioned on the shelf behind. After a hurried look around the cabin, the political commissar indicated that I could proceed!

suffered for having two children. During his eighteen years in the Navy, Captain Wu told me he had served on six ships. Meanwhile, the Political Commissar sat quietly observing everything and listening; should I have asked any awkward questions, I have no doubt that he would have quickly deflected them. We ate a deliciously simple lunch of rice, chicken, fresh mushrooms, bamboo shoots and fish soup. To drink, there was beer and fruit juice.

Captain Wu, accompanied by his Political Commissar and Deputy Captain, walked with me to the top of the gangway and, in his quiet way, shook my hand and said goodbye. Before stepping into the car I turned round and waved. Each man gave a gentle wave in return. As we drove through the maze of jetties and berths, I caught a final glimpse of the J121 outlined by a small patch of sunlight against the rain-threatening sky. During the drive back to the hotel, Mr Gu reminded me that our seats had been confirmed on a China Airways flight for the following day. My next destination was Dalian, on the tip of the Liaodong Peninsula in Liaoning Province, that part of North-East China once known as Manchuria, an area of constant conflict until the establishment of Communist

In the men's dining quarters young conscript sailors hurriedly consume their lunch of rice, chicken and vegetables after a busy morning's work. About a hundred crew members can be fed at any one time in this dining room, at six-place tables.

189

China. Alien powers came and went with alarming frequency, among them the Japanese and the Russians. During the Chinese Civil War, the Red Army in Manchuria, under the leadership of Lin Biao, fought some of its bitterest battles and totally routed the Kuomintang who were attempting to relieve the city of Mukden, known today as Shenyang.

Our plane was over an hour late, due, we were told, to bad weather. It was late in the afternoon before the Fokker Friendship (F27) eventually headed north over the Bo Hai Gulf, on the final part of my journey. In the seats behind, two English-speaking passengers were commiserating with each other about the problems of the flight. 'Forget airline schedules in China,' one of them remarked. 'Out here you fly China time.'

Dalian is the 'Lands End' of Liaoning Province; it is an ice-free port and a busy oil terminal; sandwiched between the Bo Hai Gulf and Korea Bay, it is roughly the half-way point between the Chinese mainland and North Korea. In its time, Dalian has been known by a variety of names: Dairen and Luda are the better known ones. Down at the very tip of the Liaodong Peninsula are the naval

Future naval officers at work in one of the large lecture theatres at the Dalian Naval Academy. Many of the buildings and facilities of this thirty-year-old training establishment are being replaced; new buildings are now under construction and students are expecting to move into them during the coming year.

Computer studies play a vital part in the modernization of China's military educational programme. Here a female officer instructs a class in the use of Japanese computers.

dockyards, known at various times as Port Arthur or Lushun.

I had come to Dalian to visit the Naval Academy and see something of how the Navy was training its future admirals. In that it prepares young midshipmen for a naval career, the Academy has much in common with the Royal Navy's College at Dartmouth.

On average there are 1,800 students at the Academy who receive a four year training and graduate with a Bachelor of Arts degree. Education is paramount in the PLA's modernization programme. Everyone, from conscript to senior officer, will be expected to achieve far higher educational standards than have been required in the past.

There is a compelling awareness by the military that they must make up for lost time due to the mistakes of the Cultural Revolution which created an educational vacuum in China. Military studies are now introduced into the secondary school curriculum and some schools are offering students up to seventy hours of training in military discipline, air defence and light weapons practice over their first two years. For students considering the armed forces as a career, China has well over one hundred military institutions with facilities to train the PLA's future officers.

The Navy had made arrangements for me to stay at the Nanshan Guesthouse, a quiet hotel built for tourists and officials visiting the area. It had secluded rooms and every modern facility, including an indoor swimming pool, and nestled in a quiet suburb of Dalian, only a fifteen-minute drive away from the Academy. After I had settled in, Mr Yen, one of the senior administration officers, drove over to tell me the arrangements for my visit.

Much to my delight, the Navy had arranged a march past for me – well, it was not just for me – the Academy instructors also thought it would be an excellent opportunity for the midshipmen to practise for their graduation day! But first I would see something of the College and the academic life there; and later join the students out in the Bo Hai Gulf for one of their seamanship exercises. One of the senior lecturers at the Academy had invited me to his home to meet his wife and family. It was going to be a busy few days.

Most of my afternoon was spent in an old converted lifeboat,

Young men selected by the Navy for a career are given a rigorous four-year training at the Academy which includes general academic work, in addition to specific naval studies. Successful midshipman graduates are awarded a degree. Here young midshipmen undergo seamanship training in a small bay near to the Dalian Naval Academy.

powered by an ageing diesel engine, criss-crossing the bay. As the sea was choppy, it made my task of photographing the young midshipmen, rowing tirelessly up and down the coast, a demanding one. In spite of the lovely weather, with its cool breeze blowing across the bay, I was pleased to be back on shore.

After changing back at my hotel, we drove to the Naval Academy to keep my appointment with Mr Jin Shou Qi, a fifty-six year old navigation lecturer, and his family. The apartment block where Mr Jin lived with his wife and daughter was a dreary four-storey building. It was one of several where the five hundred faculty members had their homes, surrounding the main buildings, which comprised the Dalian Ships' Academy. We climbed the stairs to the fourth floor where the family lived. Each of the landings was piled high with extra cupboards and kitchen furniture. Several of the occupants had hung herbs out on small lines to dry.

While modest by Western standards, Mr Jin's four roomed apartment had a comfy atmosphere, with its lace curtains, shaded table lamps, books, television and hi-fi. In a Chinese household

these are expensive luxuries and I knew that this was not the lifestyle of the average home in China but one of a senior officer in the Naval Service of the PLA. Everything was neatly in its place. Even the television set on the shelf was discreetly hidden with a deep red embroidered slip-over cover – rather like granny's tea cosy.

Mr Jin spoke English – not fluently but, apart from the occasional word, well enough not to need the inimitable Mr Gu to translate for us. His wife and daughter served orange juice and melon while we all chatted about our families. Both he and his wife, Zhang Mei Rong, graduated from Nankai University and, four years later, he joined the staff of the Naval Academy as a navigation lecturer, specializing in electronic navigation. Although he had only a few more years in the Navy before retiring, Mr Jin told me he still worked a fourteen-hour day. As we munched deliciously cold slices of melon – very expensive at that time of the year – Mr Jin mentioned how much he liked dancing! It was admissions like this that showed me how much China has changed. A few years ago it would have been unthinkable for a senior naval officer to admit to doing a waltz or tango! Such behaviour was considered decadent. Now only the departed spirits of Mao and the Fathers of the Revolution would be disturbed.

It was Mr Gu who indicated to me that it was time to go. Before leaving I asked Zhang Mei Rong if I could see the family kitchen. She gently shook her head and lowered her eyes. The kitchen was not good enough for me to see – she was very sorry. The three of

them walked down the stairs with me to the car. The sky was overcast. As we drove away, I looked back through the car's rear window; Mr Jin was between his wife and daughter. In his cream-coloured tunic, he showed up sharply against the drab buildings. They stood there waving until their foreign visitor had disappeared from view round a bend in the road. Our driver started the windscreen wipers; it had begun to rain.

On my last day at the Academy two hundred midshipmen marched past for me – not once, but twice! Everyone was inspected in minute detail before the parade. The cadets were an impressive sight in their crisp, white tunics as they marched down the parade square to the music of their band. As the light was so changeable I asked the Parade Commander if the cadets would repeat the performance. After coming so far I felt there was no harm in asking. Generously, he agreed.

The following day we caught the morning flight back to Peking.

On the afternoon of my departure for London, Mr Chen and Mr Gu came to see me off. Since I had plagued Mr Gu on more than one occasion about the hazards of film going through X-ray machines, they did everything in their power to ensure that the Chinese security officers were sympathetic. As a result, my film escaped X-ray inspection. We all smiled and looked happy. Mr Chen beamed and shook my hand vigorously, saying: 'Please come back and see us – we have learnt a great deal from you.' I assured him that I also had learnt a great deal in China. Even Mr Gu was in a conciliatory mood and thought that now that it was all over, he would miss my company and continuous demands. 'We had our problems, but you were very patient with us,' he commented kindly.

Patient or not, and regardless of my inner frustrations brought about by endless officialdom, I had been very fortunate that my visit had allowed me to observe something of the formidable might of China's military, the People's Liberation Army. Modernization is the theme of the new revolution which is sweeping aside many of the doctrines once sacred to the fighters of the Long March. As a witness to this new revolution, I had been allowed to gaze into the eye of the Dragon, and had seen a red star rising...

PART 3
A SELECTION OF CONVENTIONAL WEAPONS AND EQUIPMENT: CURRENT AND UNDER DEVELOPMENT

Many Western military analysts are all too ready to point out that the PLA's weaponry is woefully outmoded and that there has been little improvement in the PLA's armoury for thirty years or more.

It would be easy enough therefore for the casual observer to assume that China is incapable of defending or arming herself. Nothing could be further from the truth.

It must be remembered that China has a flourishing arms manufacturing business: she is currently fifth in the order of world arms suppliers. China is anxious to close the gap in respect of her dated weapons inventory. So, by arranging co-production deals with other countries, China North Industries Corporation (NORINCO), together with allied companies, produce defence equipment and develop weapons for internal distribution and export. By selling her weapons on the world market – though mainly to Third World countries and the Communist Bloc – China is at the same time funding her own arms requirements.

While some of the equipment illustrated in the following pages may be familiar to my readers, other items, principally the varied selection of armoured vehicles, aircraft and ships, are either prototypes or new equipment known to be at present under development and production – principally for the export market. However, without doubt, some of these weapons are certainly being used by selected units of the People's Liberation Army.

Sub-machine-gun 7.62 mm   Type 56–1
(Kalashnikov-type assault rifle)

A sub-machine-gun for infantry and special units; it has an effective range up to four hundred metres, and fires a 7.62 mm type 56 cartridge.

SPECIAL FEATURES
Folding stock single and automatic fire.

DATA
Calibre: 7.62 mm
Muzzle velocity: 710 m/s
Effective range: 400 metres
Rate of fire:
    single shot: 40 rounds/minute
    automatic: 90–100 rounds/minute
Weapon length:
    stock folded: 645 mm
    stock extended: 874 mm
Weight (magazine empty): 3.7 kg
Magazine capacity: 30 rounds

Sub-machine-gun 7.62 mm   Type 56–2
(Kalashnikov-type assault rifle)

An ideal automatic weapon for infantry and special units. It fires 7.62 mm cartridges type 56 and has an effective range of four hundred metres.

SPECIAL FEATURES
Easy to carry, rigid, folding frame stock. High accuracy, single or fully automatic fire.

DATA
Identical to type 56–1 with the exception of:
Weapon length:
    stock folded: 654 mm
Weight (magazine empty): 3.9 kg

CQ automatic rifle 5.56 mm

This automatic/semi-automatic weapon is believed to be the first of its kind produced by NORINCO. It is light in weight with a high rate of fire, easy to operate and accurate, with a large capacity magazine.

DATA
Calibre: 5.56 mm
Muzzle velocity: 990 m/s
Effective range: 460 metres
Rate of fire:
  automatic: 150–200 rounds/minute
  semi-automatic: 12–15 rounds/minute
Length: 987 mm
Weight unloaded: 3.2 kg
Weight loaded: 3.44 kg
Magazine capacity: 20 rounds
Cartridge data:
  length: 57.4 mm
  weight: 11.6 g
  bullet weight: 3.56 g
  average velocity at 25 metres (V25): 965 m/s

Semi-automatic sniping rifle 7.62 mm

This semi-automatic sniping rifle fires 7.62 mm ball cartridges (with slug) and can be used effectively to a range of 1,000 metres.

DATA
Calibre: 7.62 mm
Muzzle velocity: 830 m/s
Effective range: 1,000 metres
Rate of fire: 30 rounds/minute
Overall length: 1,220 mm
Weight with telescope and cheek rest: 4.4 kg
Magazine capacity: 10 rounds
Telescopic sight:
  magnification: × 4
  field of view: 6°
  exit pupil: 6 mm
  eye relief: 70 mm
  graduated range: 1,000 metres
  graduated direction: ± 0 ~ 10 mils
  weight: 0.6 kg

Automatic rifle 7.62 mm   Type 81

Light machine-gun 7.62 mm   Type 81–1

The 7.62 mm automatic rifle Type 81 and light machine-gun Type 81–1 are weapons of compact construction, effective firepower, are easy to handle and have fine accuracy.

The automatic rifle Type 81 is ideally suited for airborne troops and special forces.

DATA
Calibre: 7.62 mm
Muzzle velocity:
  rifle: 720 m/s
  LMG: 735 m/s
Effective range:
  rifle: 400 metres
  LMG: 600 metres
Rate of firing combat condition at semi-automatic: 45 rounds/minute
Full automatic: 100–115 rounds/minute
Overall length:
  rifle fixed stock: 955 mm
  folding stock: 730 mm
  with bayonet: 1,105 mm
  LMG: 1,024 mm
Total weight:
  rifle, fixed stock (magazine empty): 3.4 kg
  rifle, folding stock (magazine empty): 3.5 kg
  LMG (magazine empty): 5.3 kg
Magazine capacity:
  rifle: 30 rounds (interchangeable with LMG)
  LMG: 75 rounds (interchangeable with rifle)

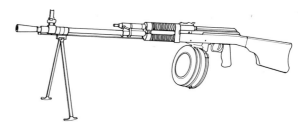

Light machine-gun 7.62 mm   Type 74

This light machine-gun is a principal infantry weapon and fires 7.62 mm cartridges Type 56.

SPECIAL FEATURES
This LMG is of simple construction, easy operation and drum-fed. The magazine for the 7.62 mm sub-machine-gun Type 56 can also be used.

DATA
Calibre: 7.62 mm
Muzzle velocity: 735 m/s
Effective range: 600 metres
Rate of fire: 150 rounds/minute
Length: 1,070 mm
Weight (drum empty): 6.2 kg
Drum capacity: 101 rounds

Light sub-machine-gun 7.62 mm   Type 79

This extremely lightweight sub-machine-gun is designed
primarily for airborne and subversive units. It fires 7.62 mm
Type 51 pistol cartridges, and has an effective range up to
200 metres.

SPECIAL FEATURES
Lightweight, small, simple construction, capable of single or
automatic fire.

DATA
Calibre: 7.62 mm
Muzzle velocity: 500 m/s
Effective range: 200 metres
Rate of fire:
   single shot: 30 rounds/minute
   automatic: 70 rounds/minute
Weapon length:
   stock folded: 470 mm
   stock extended: 740 mm
Weight (magazine empty): 1.9 kg
Magazine capacity: 20 rounds

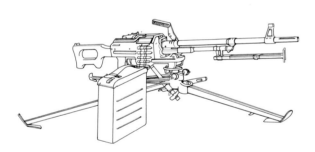

Multi-purpose machine-gun 7.62 mm   Type 80

An effective infantry weapon, this machine gun fires 7.62 mm
cartridges Type 53, with an effective range of 1,000 metres.

SPECIAL FEATURES
Lightweight, simple construction, high precision. Multi-purpose
weapon for anti-aircraft and flat trajectory fire, can be used as a light
machine-gun as well as a heavy machine-gun. Incorporated with a
flash-hider which helps to stabilize the gun at firing. Dust covers at
several positions. Rear sight is arched, making it easy to adjust for
short range.

DATA
Calibre: 7.62 mm
Muzzle velocity: 825 m/s
Effective range: 1,000 metres
Rate of fire: 350 rounds/minute
Length: 1,192 mm
Barrel length: 675 mm

Total weight (including tripod): 12.6 kg
Fire area at flat trajectory fire:
   traverse: 73°
   elevation: −13° ~ +18°
Fire area at anti-aircraft fire:
   maximum elevation: 72°
Magazine box capacity: 100 or 200 rounds

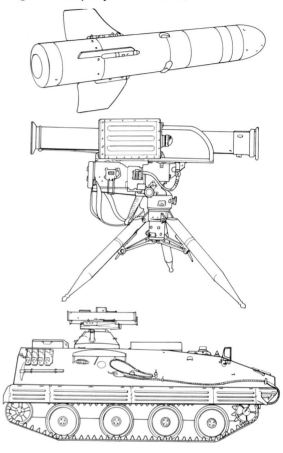

Red Arrow 8   Anti-Tank Weapon System

The Red Arrow 8 is a second generation anti-tank missile. It is
designed as an infantry weapon to be used against the
enemy's tanks and armoured vehicles within an effective
range of 100 metres to 3,000 metres.

It is a portable weapons system, which can be fired from a
kneeling position and if so desired can be mounted on
wheeled or tracked vehicles as illustrated.

The missile is tube-launched, optically-tracked, wire
command-link and semi-automatic with an infra-red guidance
system.

DATA
Effective range: 100–3,000 metres
Penetration static: >800 mm
Hit probability: > 90%
Flight velocity: 200–240 m/s
Rate of fire: 2–3 rounds/minute
Warhead diameter: 120 mm

Length: 875 mm
Weight: 11.2 kg
Wing span: 320 mm
**Weight of launcher
   (tripod):** 47 kg

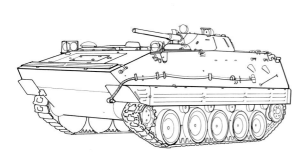

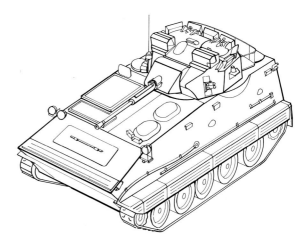

Infantry Combat Vehicle   Type YW 309

This Infantry Combat Vehicle is mainly used to transport infantrymen and accompanying tanks, as well as carrying out an individual fighting role. It may also be used to transport goods and ammunition.

This is a vehicle that has the potential to knock out enemy tanks, light armoured vehicles and anti-tank emplacements. It is an amphibious vehicle that has good manoeuvrability, with an infantry compartment, firing ports and sighting equipment.

PERFORMANCE AND TECHNICAL INFORMATION
Crew (Passengers): 3 (8)
Length: 6,270 mm
Width: 3,060 mm
Height: 2,475 mm
Tread: 2,526 mm
Length of track on ground: 3,275 mm
Ground clearance: 467 mm
Maximum speed: 65 km/h
Average speed on highway: 40–50 km/h
Average speed on country road: 35 km/h
Maximum range: 500 km
Maximum gradient: 32°
Maximum sideslope: 25°
Speed in water: 6 km/h

Main Armament: 73 mm smooth-bore low-pressure gun with forty rounds of ammunition stowed.
  ammunition type: AT HE
  traverse: 360°

Other Armament: A 7.62 mm machine-gun; sighting and vision devices; day periscope; day and night sight for the gunner; day and night periscope for the driver; equipped with radio communications.

Infantry Combat Vehicle   NVH1

A highly effective infantry fighting vehicle at present in its prototype stage, to be constructed jointly between Britain's Vickers Defence Systems at Newcastle-upon-Tyne and China North Industries Corporation for export purposes.

Vickers have designed the turret for this vehicle and the Chinese have designed the chassis.

PERFORMANCE AND TECHNICAL INFORMATION
Combat weight: 16 tons
Maximum speed: 65 km/h
Maximum range: 500+ km
Maximum gradient: 31°
Maximum sideslope: 25°
Carrying capacity: Driver, two in turret, plus six

Dimensions:
  length: 6,125 mm
  width: 3,060 mm
  height: 2,770 mm

Armament: 25 mm M242 automatic cannon
  ammunition type: APDS, HEI
  rate of fire: single or 200 rounds/minute
  traverse (electric or manual): 360°
  ammunition storage: 500 rounds × 25 mm
  secondary armament (co-axial): 7.62 mm chain gun
  ammunition stowage: 2,000 × 7.62 mm
  grenade discharger: 66 mm – 4 barrels/side

Engine: A Deutz, air-cooled, turbo-charged and inter-cooled
  rated engine power at 2,500 rpm: 320 hp
  gear box: Five forward, one reverse
  suspension: Torsion bar, linear dampers

Commanders and Gunners Sights:
  type: NVL 53, linked to gun
  field of view: 8° and 25°
  night vision: Image intensifying with optional TI module for gunner or commander
  magnification: X 8 and X I

Additional Vision Equipment:
  vision blocks: Seven in turret, nine in hull
  driver's night vision: Infra-red projector (image intensifying optional)
  commander or gunner's periscope: one rotating, mounted centrally

Navigation Equipment: GEC Avionics Land Navigation System.

122 mm Howitzer   Type 54–1

This mobile Howitzer is capable of firing with a high or flat trajectory whilst on the move. It is fitted with an IR night vision device for the driver.

DATA
Combat loaded weight: 15.3 tons
Crew (passengers): 2 (5)
Maximum road speed: 56 km/h
Maximum range: 450 km
Maximum gradient: 25°
Engine: A six cylinder in-line four cycle water-cooled diesel
Maximum output: 260 hp
Speed at maximum output: 2,000 rpm
Front armour: 12 mm giving protection against 7.62 mm armour piercing at 300 m
Weapons: 122 mm Howitzer Type 54–1 [one 7.62 mm multipurpose machine-gun with 1,000 rounds of stowed ammunition. Communications equipment capable of 16 km]
  calibre: 121.99 mm
  muzzle velocity: 515 m/s
  maximum range: 11,800 metres
  point blank range (full charge): 600 metres
  maximum rate of fire: 5 rounds/minute
  elevation: −25° ~ +63°
  traverse: Approx 22.5°
  ammunition stowed: Forty rounds

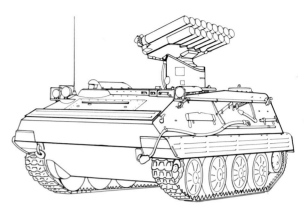

Rocket launcher   Type 70 130 mm

This nineteen tube rocket launcher has good cross-country performance and is capable of travelling at high speeds. The vehicle has some armour protection and can produce a high firing density in a relatively short space of time. It has good manoeuvrability with a wide range of elevation.

PERFORMANCE AND TECHNICAL INFORMATION
Combat loaded weight: 13.4 tons
Crew: 6
Maximum speed: 60 km/h
Maximum range: 500 km
Maximum gradient: 32°
Maximum sideslope: 25°
Maximum speed in water: 5.2 km/h
Weapons: One 130 mm Rocket Launcher Type 70
  calibre: 130.65 mm
  elevation: 0~50°
  maximum range: 10,370 metres
  rate of fire: 19 rounds in 9.5~11.5 seconds
  time required from travelling to firing: Approx 2 minutes
  time required from firing to travelling: Approx 1 minute
Engine: 6 cylinder in-line four cycle water-cooled diesel
  maximum output: 260 hp
  speed at maximum output: 2,000 rpm
Radio communications: To a distance of 16 km
Front armour thickness: 12 mm, giving protection against 7.62 mm AP at 300 metres

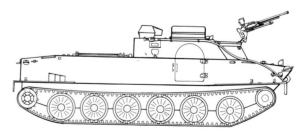

Amphibious Armoured Vehicle   Type 77–2

This amphibious armoured vehicle is a personnel and supplies carrier and is capable of operations in all water environments. It can also be used as a command post. It is a high speed vehicle, easy to operate, with a spacious troop compartment.

PERFORMANCE & TECHNICAL INFORMATION
Weight: 15.5 tons
Maximum travelling speed:
   on land: 60 km/h
   in water: 12 km/h
Maximum range:
   highway travel and country roads: 370 km
   in water: 120 km
Maximum gradient: 38°
Maximum sideslope: 32°
Carrying capacity:
   payload: 3 tons
   personnel: 16

Dimensions:
   length: 7,400 mm
   width: 3,200 mm
   height (to AA MG at horizontal position): 2,436 mm
   length of track on ground: 4,440 mm
   tread: 2,820 mm
   ground clearance: 400 mm

Armament: One 12.7 mm AA machine-gun with five hundred rounds
   of ammunition stowed
Engine: A four-cycle, direct injection and water-cooled diesel
   power output: 400 hp
   maximum speed: 2,000 rpm

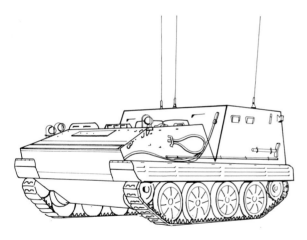

Armoured Command Vehicle   Type WZ 701

A communication and command post vehicle, which can also
work in conjunction with tank forces, this is a high speed
armoured vehicle with cross-country ability and excellent
communication facilities. It is fitted with five radio sets (two of
which are reserves), manual radio-signal converting device
and line remote-controlled intercom for the commander to
use the radio set when dismounting. Also included is an
auxiliary power supply, battery commander's telescope and
operational drawing board for map use. The command room
has twelve viewing ports with defrosting equipment. It is also
fitted with forced ventilation facilities, fans and heaters. The
driving compartment is fitted with an IR system.

PERFORMANCE & TECHNICAL INFORMATION
Combat loaded weight: 13 tons
Maximum speed: 60 km/h
Crew (passengers): 3 (5)
Reserve seats: 2
Maximum gradient: 32°
Maximum sideslope: 25°
Travelling speed in water: 6 km/h
Fording depth: 1.5 metres
Engine: In-line, six cylinder, four-cycle, water-cooled diesel
Maximum output: 260 hp
Speed at maximum output: 2,000 rpm
Weapon: 7.62mm light machine-gun, complete with 1,000 rounds of
   ammunition
Front armour thickness: 12 mm

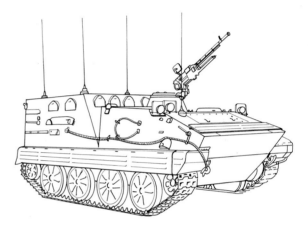

Armoured Command Vehicle   Type YW 701A

This vehicle has similar features to that of the WZ701 but with
improved mobility and communications performance. It is
fitted with two ulta-short-wave FM radiosets and one short-
wave side band radio. It comes equipped with two reserve
radios and has a communications distance of 30~5 km.

Engine: Four cycle, turbo-charged and inter-cooled V8 air-cooled
   diesel type BF 8L 413F, an engine suitable for desert operations.
   Its maximum output is 320hp. The vehicle is equipped with five
   small cooling fans, for crew and passengers.
Weapon: One 12.7 mm AA machine-gun, with accommodation for
   560 rounds.

Armoured Personnel Carrier   Type YW 531H

This armoured personnel carrier has a good cross-country ability and some armoured protection and is equipped with anti-aircraft weaponry. The vehicle is powered by an air-cooled engine suitable for desert areas. It comes equipped with IR night vision for the driver. Its tracks are double-pinned rubber-bushed complete with rubber pads making it capable of road travel.

PERFORMANCE & TECHNICAL INFORMATION
Crew (passengers): 2 (13)
Length: 5,900 mm
Width: 3,060 mm
Height to top of MG: 2,586 mm
Combat loaded weight: 13.6 tons
Ground clearance: 460 mm
Engine: Four cycle air-cooled diesel
Maximum power output: 320 hp
Maximum speed: 65 km/h
Mean speed on the road: 40–45 km/h
Mean speed on country road: 35 km/h
Maximum range: 500 km
Maximum gradient: 32°
Maximum side-slope: 25°
Speed in water: 6 km/h
Armament: 12.7 mm AA machine-gun equipped with 1,120 rounds of ammunition; radio and intercom.

The Main Battle Tank   T69–II

This is one of the most up-to-date tanks being produced in China and although the T69–II Battle Tank is regarded as being constructed primarily for export purposes, it is inconceivable that the PLA is not in possession of at least a limited number of them. More than likely these tanks would be supporting troops along the sensitive Russian and Vietnamese borders.

The tank is fitted with an advanced fire control system and IR night vision. It is also reported as being fitted with a Type 889 radio which the Chinese claim is superior to the Soviet Type R123.

PERFORMANCE & TECHNICAL INFORMATION
Combat loaded weight: 36.5~37 tons
Engine power output: 580 hp
Crew: 4
Maximum road speed: 50 km/h
Range: 420~440 km
Maximum gradient: 32°
Maximum side-slope: 30°
Fording depth: 1.4 metres
Weapons: One 100 mm rifled gun; one 12.7 mm AA MG; two 7.62 mm MG
Ammunition: AP, HE, HEAT and HVAPDS
Fire Control System: This includes a laser range-finder, ballistics calculator and aiming sight with stepping motor. The firing table is automatically fed into the gun and the firing angle provided. The gun is stabilized in elevation and azimuth.
Observation Equipment: Commander's vision block Type 69
Magnification:
   day: X 5
   night: X 6
Target recognition range: 350 metres
Field of View:
   day: 12°
   night: 8°

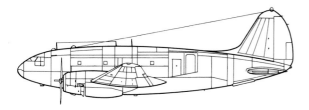

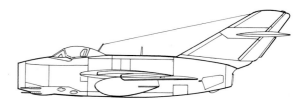

The C46 – Curtiss-Wright Commando

(Affectionately called 01' Dumbo, Conqueror)

The Chinese Airforce inherited a number of these veteran cargo aircraft from the Nationalists following their defeat and retreat to Taiwan in 1949.

Originally, the C46 Commando was designed as a thirty-six passenger aircraft by Curtiss-Wright in 1937. During the Second World War the American Army Airforce used them to fly supplies to the Chinese Nationalist Forces over the 'Hump', the nickname given by the pilots to the mountain ranges between Northern India and the Chinese city of Kunming. The aircraft could operate at altitudes in excess of 24,000 feet, and its 2,300 cubic foot cargo hold could carry four tons of supplies.

For the C46 pilots flying the 'Hump' the flight had more than its fair share of hazards: during the tropical rains, the fuselage leaked at high altitudes, defrosters malfunctioned and fuel lines were constantly breaking, spraying petrol onto hot engines. Because there were so many wrecked Commandos scattered across the 'Hump' the countryside along the route was frequently referred to as the 'aluminium trail'.

TECHNICAL INFORMATION
Dimensions:
  wing span: 108 ft 1 in
  length: 76 feet 4 in
  wing area: 1,360 sq ft
Weights and Loadings:
  empty weight: 29,483 lbs
  loaded: 45,000 lbs
Power Plant: Two 2,000 hp Pratt and Whitney R-2800-51 Double Wasp 18-cylinder radial air-cooled engines on steel tube mountings
Total fuel capacity in the wings: 1,400 US gallons; an additional 800 US gallons can be carried in eight fuselage tanks
Accommodation: Pilot, co-pilot, navigator, radio operator; main compartment can carry forty fully-armed troops seated, in addition to general cargo

Mikoyan MiG15   Type S

The MiG15 is one of the most important combat aircraft of the post-war era. US fighter pilots came into contact with the MiG15 during the Korean War 1950–3. At that time, it was capable of out-manoeuvring the US pilots, who were flying F86 Sabres. Five hundred of these aircraft are reported to be still in operation with the PLAAF. The MiG15 UTI, a dual-control aircraft, has been specially adapted for training purposes.

TECHNICAL INFORMATION
Dimensions:
  wing span: 33 ft 7/8 ins
  length: 32 ft 11¼ ins
  wing area: 221.74 sq ft
Weights and Loadings:
  empty equipped: 7,456 lbs
  normal loading (clean): 10,595 lbs
Power Plant: One 5,005 lb thrust RD-45F single-shaft centrifugal turbojet
Power Plant (training version): One 5,952 lb thrust turbojet
Performance:
  maximum speed (at sea level): 652 mph
  maximum speed (at 9,848 ft): 648 mph
  maximum speed (at 16,405 ft): 640 mph
Range:
  at 236 mph, at 39,370 ft: 882 miles
  with 2 X 54.4 imperial gallon drop tanks: 1,192 miles
  initial climb: 8,268 ft/min
Armament: One 37 mm cannon with forty rounds; two 23 mm cannon with 80 rpg; two underwing hardpoints for tanks or stores

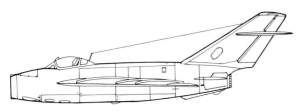

MIKOYAN MiG17 (Chinese J5)

There are an estimated four hundred Chinese versions of the MiG17 operating with the PLAAF. They have designated it the J5. The NATO codename is FRESCO, and export models are referred to as F5.

There is also a dual-controlled training version of this aircraft.

TECHNICAL INFORMATION
Dimensions:
   wing span: 31 ft
   length: 36 ft 3 ins
   wing area: 243.25 sq ft
Weights and Loading:
   empty: 8,995 lbs
   normally loaded: 11,907 lbs
   maximum loaded: 13,701 lbs
Power Plant: One 5,952 lb thrust Klimov single-shaft centrifugal turbojet; later versions have one 4,732/4,752 lb thrust turbojet with after-burner.
Performance:
   maximum speed (at 9,840 ft): 711 mph
   maximum speed (at medium heights): 651 mph
   cruising speed: 482 mph
   initial climb: 12,795 ft/min
   service ceiling: 54,460 ft
Range including drop tanks: 913 miles
Armament: As MiG15; all later versions had three 23 mm cannon; four wing hardpoints for tanks, bombs and air-to-air rockets or various air-to-ground missiles.

MIKOYAN MiG19S

There are an estimated three thousand Chinese versions of the MiG19S aircraft operating with the PLAAF, designated the J6 (NATO codename FARMER) and F6 for the export model. There is a training version of this aircraft and it is designated the JJ6.

TECHNICAL INFORMATION
Dimensions:
   wing span (excluding probe): 30 ft 2.2 ins
   length (excluding probe): 41 ft 4 ins
   wing area: 269.1 sq ft
Weights and Loading:
   empty: 12,700 lbs
   loaded – two tanks: 19,764 lbs
   maximum loading: 22,046 lbs

Power Plant: Two Tumansky R-9BF-811 turbojets each rated at 7,167 lbs thrust with after-burner.
Performance:
   maximum speed (typical) at 20,000 ft: 920 mph (Mach 1.3)
   initial climb: 22,640 ft/min
   service ceiling: 58,725 ft
Range including drop tanks: 1,367 miles
Armament: Three 30 mm cannon with 55 rpg for fuselage mounted gun and 75 rpg for wing root weapons. The aircraft is also designed to carry bombs, rocket launchers and single rockets.

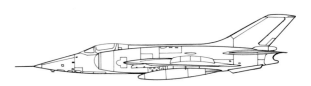

NANCHANG Q5/A5 FANTAN FIGHTER/BOMBER

There are an estimated six hundred of these aircraft in operation with the PLAAF, of which one hundred are known to be flying with the Naval Airforce. It has the NATO codename FANTAN and the export version is designated the A5.

TECHNICAL INFORMATION
Dimensions:
   wing span: 31 ft 10 ins
   length (including nose probe): 53 ft 4 ins
   wing area: 300.85 sq ft
Weight when empty: 14,317 lbs
Accommodation: Pilot only, in pressurized cockpit
Armament: One 23 mm cannon (internal) with 100 rounds in each wing root: wing mountings for 500 lb or 750 lb bomb, 600 lb cluster bomb or 25 lb practice bombs; normal bomb carrying capacity 2,205 lbs. There are wing mountings for rockets and air-to-air missiles and this aircraft can also carry a single 5–20 KT nuclear bomb.

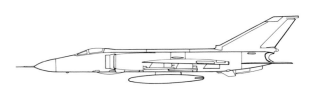

SHENJANG J8

There are an estimated thirty J8s in operation with the PLAAF. This Mach 2 aircraft, an enlarged version of the MiG21, is China's most advanced fighter and is designated the F8 for export purposes.

Development of the J8 began in the 1960s: only a limited number of the early models, some fifty in all, were constructed. Recently this aircraft has been updated by the addition of a modern avionics system supplied by the United States government, which has given it an air superiority over that of neighbouring countries.

TECHNICAL INFORMATION
Dimensions:
  wing span: 30 ft 7/8 ins
  length: 70 ft 10 ins
Power Plant: Wopen 13A II turbojet engines (Chinese development of Tumansky R-13-300) rated at 14,550 lb thrust
Fuel Capacity: 1,453 US gals; provision for auxiliary tanks on fuselage and wings
Accommodation: Pilot only, in pressurized cockpit
Armament: One 23 mm Type 23–3 twin-barrel cannon with 200 rounds; wing mountings for air-to-air missiles, air-to-air rockets, bombs and fuel tanks.

TUPOLEV TU16 MEDIUM BOMBER (Chinese H6)

There are an estimated 120 Chinese-produced copies of the Tupolev Tu16s, NATO codename BADGER, known to be in operation with the PLAAF. Recent information suggests that it would serve as a tanker aircraft for in-flight refuelling operations serving the A5 Fantan. Designated the H6, deliveries of this aircraft commenced in China in 1968.

TECHNICAL INFORMATION
Dimensions:
  wing span (information denotes that this can vary): 110 ft
  length (basic-varies with radar or glazed nose): 120 ft
  height: 35 ft 6 ins
Weight when empty: approx 72,750 lbs
Performance:
  clean at height: 587 mph
  initial climb – clean: approx 4,100 ft/min
  service ceiling: 42,650 ft
  range with maximum weapon load, no missiles: 3,000 miles
  extreme reconnaissance range: approx 4,500 miles
Armament: Six 23 mm cannon (combined radar/manned operation). In the absence of nose radar, a fixed seventh cannon firing ahead on right side of nose. Capable of carrying a 19,800 lb load. Some models are equipped to launch missiles.

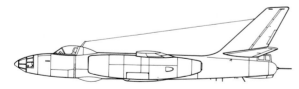

ILYUSHIN II28 LIGHT BOMBER (Chinese H5)

There are an estimated five hundred Chinese-produced copies of the Ilyushin II28 bomber, designated the H5, NATO codename BEAGLE, known to be in operation with the PLAAF. It has been in service for more than thirty years and the Chinese are reported to have no immediate replacement for it. There is also a naval version capable of carrying torpedoes.

TECHNICAL INFORMATION
Dimensions:
  wing span (without tip tanks): 70 ft 4 ins
  length: 57 ft 10¾ ins
  height: 22 ft
Weight:
  empty: 28,417 lbs
  maximum loaded: 46,297 lbs
Power Plant: Two 5,952 lb thrust Klimov single shaft centrifugal turbojets
Performance:
  maximum speed: 559 mph
  initial climb: 2,953 ft/min
  service ceiling: 40,355 ft
  range with bomb load: 684 miles
Armament: Two 23 mm cannons fixed in nose; two 23 mm cannons in power tail turret. Internal bomb capacity: 2,205 lbs

MIKHAIL Mi6 HEAVY TRANSPORT HELICOPTER

There are an estimated four hundred helicopters in service with the PLAAF, including this Chinese copy of the Soviet Mi6, NATO codename HOOK. Other helicopters in use include the Alouette 3, the Super Frelon and the Sikorsky S–70.

TECHNICAL INFORMATION
Dimensions:
  main rotor diameter: 114 ft 10 ins
  fuselage length: 108 ft 10½ ins
  height: 32 ft 4 ins
Weight:
  empty: 60,055 lbs
  maximum loaded: 93,700 lbs
Power Plant: Two 5,500 shp Soloviev single-shaft free-turbine engines driving common R7 gear box
Performance:
  maximum speed: 186 mph
  service ceiling: 14,750 ft
  range with half pay load: 404 miles
Armament: Sometimes seen with a manually-aimed 12.7 mm nose gun

Principal information source: *Jane's All the World's Aircraft*

LUDA CLASS DESTROYER

This Chinese-designed destroyer is similar to the Soviet Kotlin class. There are an estimated eleven Type 051 Luda class destroyers in service armed with HY2 SSM.

TECHNICAL INFORMATION
Displacement: 3,250 tons
Dimensions: 430 × 45 × 15 feet
Missiles: SSM Six HY2s
Guns: Four 130 mm (twin); eight 37 mm (twin) or 57 mm (twin); eight 25 mm (twin); miscellaneous selection of anti-submarine weapons
Mines: Fitted to lay up to ninety mines
Main engines: Geared turbines. Two shafts: 66,000 shp
Speed: 32 knots
Fuel: 850 tons
Range in miles: 5,000 at 14 knots. 11,000 at 32 knots
Crew: 350
Selection of radar and sonar equipment

JIANGHU CLASS FRIGATE

There are twenty Type 037 Jianghu class frigates of the thirty-one frigates reported to be in service with the Chinese Navy.

TECHNICAL INFORMATION
Displacement: 1,570 tons
Dimensions: 338.5 × 38.5 × 10.2 feet
Aircraft: One helicopter
Missiles: SSM Four HY2
Guns: Two 100 mm (single); two 2.3 in (single); four 3.9 in (twin) and others; miscellaneous selection of anti-submarine weapons
Mines: Capable of laying up to sixty mines
Main engines: Two diesels 24,000 shp, equal to 26.5 knots
Range in miles: 4,000 at 15 knots
Crew: 195

JIANGAN CLASS FRIGATE

This is similar to the Soviet Riga class. Four of these vessels are reported to be with the South Sea Fleet and one with the East Sea Fleet.

TECHNICAL INFORMATION
Displacement: 1,150 tons
Dimensions: 300.1 × 33.1 × 10.5 feet
Guns: Three 3.9 in (one forward, two aft); eight 37 mm (twin); four 14.5 mm (twin); selection of anti-submarine weapons
Mines: Ability to lay up to sixty mines
Speed: 28 knots
Range in miles: 3,000 at 10 knots; 900 at 26 knots
Crew: 180

DAJIANG SUBMARINE SUPPORT SHIP

There are an estimated ten submarine support ships, which include a repair ship, in service with the People's Liberation Army Navy (PLAN). They are equipped with light machine-guns, a helicopter deck and hangar for two aircraft.

TECHNICAL INFORMATION
Displacement (full load): 10,975 tons
Dimensions: 511.7 × 67.2 × 23 feet
Engines: Two diesels 9,000 shp equal to 20 knots

THE 'GOLF' CLASS (BALLISTIC MISSILE TYPE) SUBMARINE

These submarines are similar to the Soviet Golf class, were built at Dalian, Liaoning Province, and launched in 1974. There are twenty reported to be in service with the Chinese Navy.

TECHNICAL INFORMATION
Displacement (surfaced): 2,350 tons
Dimensions: 321.4 × 27.9 × 21 feet
Missile Launchers: Two vertical tubes in conning tower
Torpedoes: capable of carrying twelve
Engines: Three diesels, three shafts, 6,000 hp; three electric motors 12,000 hp
Speed: 17 knots surfaced, 14 knots dived
Range in miles: 22,700 on the surface
Crew: 86
Bases: Huludao and Xiaopingdao

ROMEO CLASS SUBMARINE (SS) TYPE 033

There are ninety of these submarines recorded to be on active service with the People's Liberation Army Navy. There are more submarines of this class than any other in the Navy, and they are capable of carrying fourteen torpedoes or twenty-eight mines in eight tubes.

TECHNICAL INFORMATION
Displacement (surfaced): 1,400 tons
Dimensions: 251.9 × 23.9 ×18 feet
Engines: Two diesels 4,000 hp; two electric motor 4,000 hp two
shafts
Speed: 16 knots surfaced, 13 knots dived
Range in miles: 9,000 on the surface at 9 knots
Crew: 53

THE HUANGFEN MISSILE ATTACK BOAT

A building programme was reported to be underway on these craft in 1985 and now there are 120 in service with the Chinese Navy. They are slightly smaller than the Soviet OSA class equivalent. Each boat has a selection of radar and communications equipment.

TECHNICAL INFORMATION
Displacement: 165 tons standard; 210 tons full load
Dimensions: 127.9 ×26.6 × 5.9 feet
Missiles: SSM, four HY2s (single launchers)
Guns: Four 25 mm or 30 mm (two twin, one forward, one aft)
Engines: Three diesels 12,000 bhp equalling 38–41 knots
Range in miles: 800 at 30 knots
Crew: 28

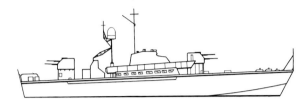

THE P6 MOTOR TORPEDO BOAT

Most of these craft were built in Shanghai shipyards prior to 1966. All have wooden hulls. There are sixty reported to be in service with the Chinese Navy. The P6 has two torpedo tubes and can also be used for mine laying; it also carries eight DCs (depth charges).

TECHNICAL INFORMATION
Displacement: 64 tons standard; 73 tons full load
Dimensions: 85.3 × 20 × 4.9 feet
Guns: Four 25 mm (twin)
Engines: Four M50 diesels capable of delivering a speed of 41 knots
Range in miles: 450 at 30 knots
Crew: 15

Principal information source: *Jane's Fighting Ships*

PAY SCALES for the PLA

Officers receive a monthly salary, whereas conscripted fighters are given a monthly allowance. The State believes that soldiers are obliged to serve the Motherland and should not be compensated for doing so. Conscripts do not receive annual leave during their term of service other than for compassionate reasons. There are, however, special allowances for troops who serve in remote areas of China or who may be serving for long periods at sea. Those fighters with specialist skills are also believed to be paid an additional allowance.

There are twenty-four different pay categories for cadres, political commissars and commanders, with the lowest grade student officer being classified on the pay scale as Number Twenty-Four.

Families experiencing hardship resulting from a member of the family conscripted to serve in the PLA, may receive compensation.

The following pay scales are only an estimate, as the Chinese authorities are reluctant to supply any information concerning renumeration for their military personnel.

YEARS IN SERVICE	POSITION/RANK	BASIC MONTHLY PAY	UK EQUIVALENT
1	Conscript	21 yuan	£4.46
2	Fighter	24 yuan	£5.10
3	Deputy Squad Leader	27 yuan	£5.94
4	Squad Leader	33 yuan	£7.02
4+	Deputy Platoon Leader	33 yuan†	£7.02 (+ £3.19)

† increased by 15 yuan each year after 4 years in service

PAY GRADE	POSITION/RANK	BASIC MONTHLY PAY*	UK EQUIVALENT
1	Vice Chairman, Military Commission	1,425 yuan	£303.19
4	Military Region Commander	1,050 yuan	£223.40
11	Army Commander	675 yuan	£143.60
13	Division Commander	570 yuan	£121.20
15	Regiment Commander	480 yuan	£102.12
19	Battalion Commander	390 yuan	£ 82.97
21	Company Commander	225 yuan	£ 47.87
23	Platoon Leader	150 yuan	£ 31.91
24	Student/Officer Trainee	135 yuan	£ 28.72

* Estimated monthly basic pay including longevity increments

Political Structure of China

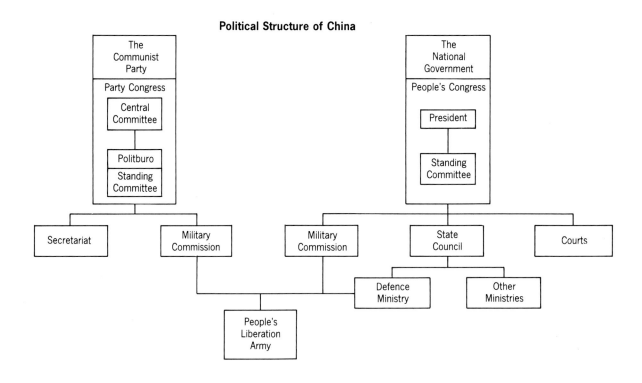

Military Organization of China

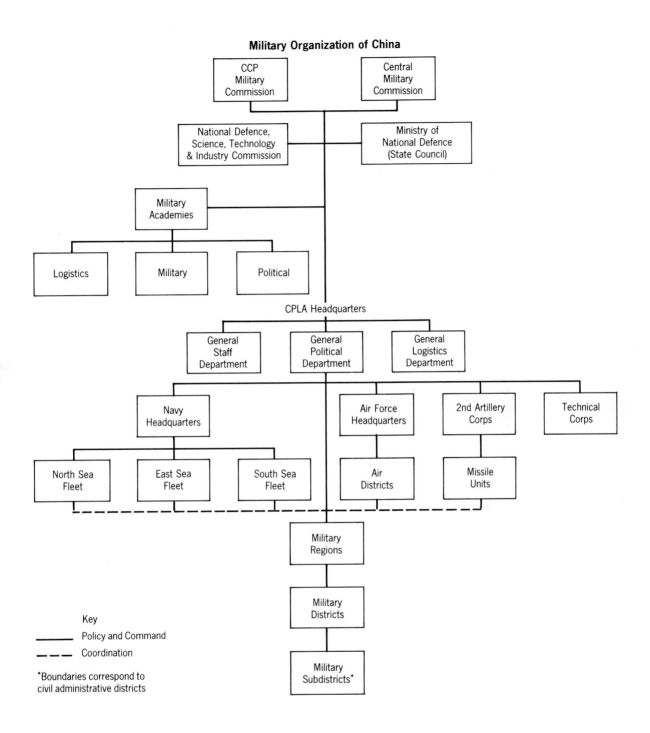

Key

───── Policy and Command

- - - Coordination

*Boundaries correspond to
civil administrative districts

Organization of an Army

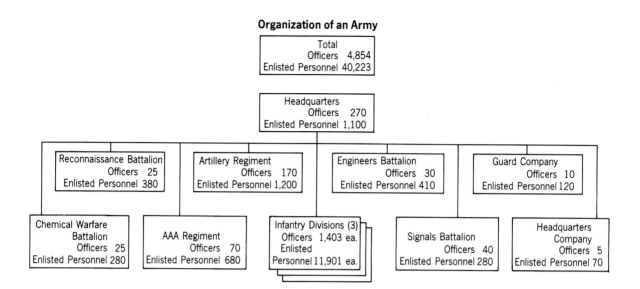

Table of Personnel and Major Equipment

Personnel/Equipment	Total Army	Hq Army	Hq Co	Recon Bn	Engr Bn	Sig Bn	CW Bn	Gd Co	AAA Regt	Arty Regt	Three Inf Div
Officers	4,854	270	5	25	30	40	25	10	70	170	4,209
Enlisted Personnel	40,223	1,100	70	380	410	280	280	120	680	1,200	35,703
Total Personnel	45,077	1,370	75	405	440	320	305	130	750	1,370	39,912
7.62mm LMG	1,087			30	30			10			1,017
7.62/12.7mm HMG	216										216
40mm Antitank Grenade Launcher (RPG)	1,558+			X	X			10			1,548+
57/75/82mm Recoilless Rifle	162										162
60/82/120/160mm Mortar	441										441
76/85/100mm Field Gun	54										54
122mm Howitzer	46									10	36
122/130mm Field Gun	10									10	
152mm Gun Howitzer	10									10	
130mm Rocket Launcher	72									18	54
14.5mm AAHMG	46								10		36
37/57mm AA Gun	79								25		54
Tank, Medium	240										240
APC	42										42
ARV	15										15
Truck, Cargo/Prime Mover	1,464	120	15	2	13	3	2		90	100	1,119
Artillery Tractor/Truck, Prime Mover	24									24	
CW Equipment, Various	X						X				X
Flamethrower	81										81
Boat Inflatable, 4-10 man	X			X	X						X
Bridging Material	X				X						X
Radio Portable/Manpack	1,383+	X	X	20	3	25	X	X	40	80	1,215
Radio, Vehicle Mounted	248+	X	X	7	X	4	X	X	X	X	237

X = Amount of equipment not available

Organization of an Infantry Division

```
                    ┌─────────────────────────┐
                    │           Total          │
                    │     Officers    1,403    │
                    │ Enlisted Personnel 11,961│
                    └─────────────────────────┘
                    ┌─────────────────────────┐
                    │       Headquarters       │
                    │      Officers 133        │
                    │ Enlisted Personnel 493   │
                    └─────────────────────────┘
```

- 107mm Recoilless Rifle Company
- Chemical Warfare Company — Officers 10, Enlisted Personnel 90
- Artillery Regiment — Officers 150, Enlisted Personnel 985
- AAAW Battalion — Officers 52, Enlisted Personnel 463
- Signals Battalion — Officers 48, Enlisted Personnel 270
- Headquarters Company — Officers 7, Enlisted Personnel 63
- Flame-thrower Company — Officers 9, Enlisted Personnel 75
- Reconnaissance Company — Officers 10, Enlisted Personnel 125
- Engineers Battalion — Officers 40, Enlisted Personnel 491
- Guard Company — Officers 9, Enlisted Personnel 96
- Tank Regiment — Officers 182, Enlisted Personnel 1,112
- Infantry Regiments (3) — Officers 251 ea., Enlisted Personnel 2,566 ea.

Table of Personnel and Major Equipment

Personnel/Equipment	Total Inf Div	Hq Inf Div	Hq Co	Recon Co	Engr Bn	Sig Bn	AAAW Bn	CW Co	FT Co	Gd Co	Tank Regt	Arty Regt	Three Inf Regts (Total)
Officers	1,403	133	7	10	40	48	52	10	9	9	182	150	753
Enlisted Personnel	11,961	493	63	125	491	270	463	90	75	96	1,112	985	7,698
Total Personnel	13,364	626	70	135	531	318	515	100	84	105	1,294	1,135	8,451
7.62mm LMG	339				9	27					6		297
7.62mm HMG	54												54
12.7mm HMG	18												18
40mm Antitank Grenade Launcher (RPG)	516+	48			X	X				X			468
57/75/82mm Recoilless Rifle	54												54
60mm Mortar	54												54
82mm Mortar	81												81
120/160mm Mortar	12											12	
85mm Field Gun	18											18	
122mm Howitzer	12												
130mm Rocket Launcher	18												
14.5mm AAHMG	12						12						
37/57mm AA Gun	18						18						
Tank, Medium	80										80		
APC	14										14		
ARV	5										5		
Truck, Cargo/Prime Mover*	373+	67	12		15+	3	60				29	97	90
Motorcycle w/Sidecar	44+			9	4	X		5			12	5	9
CW Equipment, Various	X				X			X			X		X
Flamethrower	27								27				
Radio, Manpack/Portable	405			8	5	21	31				18	70	252

✕ = Amount of equipment not available
* Includes 6 ambulances

Organization of a Tank Division

Organization of a Tank Division

Total
Officers 1,258
Enlisted Personnel 8,621

Headquarters
Officers 119
Enlisted Personnel 371

Reconnaissance Battalion
Officers 32
Enlisted Personnel 392

*Artillery Regiment
Officers 155
Enlisted Personnel 1,000

Engineers Battalion
Officers 40
Enlisted Personnel 482

Guard Company
Officers 9
Enlisted Personnel 96

Chemical Warfare Company
Officers 10
Enlisted Personnel 90

AAA Battalion
Officers 52
Enlisted Personnel 421

Signals Battalion
Officers 48
Enlisted Personnel 270

Headquarters Company
Officers 7
Enlisted Personnel 63

Tank Regiments (3)
Officers 182 ea.
Enlisted Personnel 1,112 ea.

*Mechanized Infantry Division
Officers 240
Enlisted Personnel 2,100

* Not all tank divisions have mechanized infantry and artillery regiments.

Table of Personnel and Major Equipment

Personnel/Equipment	Total Tank Div	Hq Tank Div	Hq Co	Recon Bn	Sig Bn	Engr Bn	AAA Bn	Gd Co	CW Co	Arty Regt*	Mech Inf Regt*	Three Tank Regts (Total)*
Officers	1,258	119	7	32	48	40	52	9	10	155	240	546
Enlisted Personnel	8,621	371	63	392	270	482	421	96	90	1,000	2,100	3,336
Total Personnel	9,879	490	70	424	318	522	473	105	100	1,155	2,340	3,882
7.62mm LMG	125			10		30		5			80	
12.7 HMG	5										5	
40mm Antitank Grenade Launcher (RPG)	156+			X		X		X			156	
57/75mm Recoilless Rifle	8										8	
75/82mm Recoilless Rifle	9										9	
60mm Mortar	15										15	
82mm Mortar	25										25	
120/160mm Mortar	10									10		
76/85/100mm Field Gun	20	X								20		
122mm Howitzer	12									12		
14.5mm AAHMG	12						12					
37/57mm AA Gun	18						18					
Tank, Medium	241	1										240
Armoured Recovery Vehicle	20			5								15
Armoured Personnel Carrier	139			12							85	42
Light Tank	12			12								
Truck, Cargo*	535	50	10		5	10	50			90	80	240
Truck, ¼–½ ton	72	5	10		1	1				5	20	30
Wrecker	8	1								2	5	
Motorcycle w/Sidecar	58					3			3	3	19	30
CW Equipment, Various	X					X			X	X	X	X
CW Decontamination Vehicle	5								2			3
Radio, Manpack/Portable	335			10	20	5	30			60	105	105
Radio, Vehicle Mounted	628	6		6	6						100	510

X = Amount of equipment not available
* Includes 7 ambulances and 3 radio trucks

Organization of the Air Force

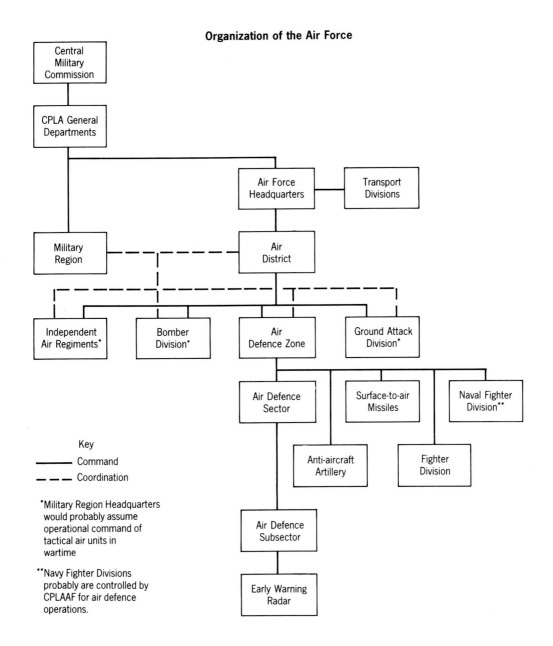

Central
Military
Commission

CPLA General
Departments

Air Force
Headquarters

Transport
Divisions

Military
Region

Air
District

Independent
Air Regiments*

Bomber
Division*

Air
Defence Zone

Ground Attack
Division*

Air Defence
Sector

Surface-to-air
Missiles

Naval Fighter
Division**

Anti-aircraft
Artillery

Fighter
Division

Air Defence
Subsector

Early Warning
Radar

Key

———— Command

— — — Coordination

*Military Region Headquarters
would probably assume
operational command of
tactical air units in
wartime

**Navy Fighter Divisions
probably are controlled by
CPLAAF for air defence
operations.

215

Organization of an Airborne Division

```
                        ┌─────────────────────────────┐
                        │            Total            │
                        │       Officers    799       │
                        │   Enlisted Personnel 8,300  │
                        └─────────────────────────────┘
                                      │
                        ┌─────────────────────────────┐
                        │        Headquarters         │
                        │        Officers  90         │
                        │   Enlisted Personnel 430    │
                        └─────────────────────────────┘
```

| Reconnaissance Company Officers 8 Enlisted Personnel 100 | AA Company Officers 8 Enlisted Personnel 90 | Guard Company Officers 8 Enlisted Personnel 90 | Artillery Battalion Officers 25 Enlisted Personnel 200 |

| Headquarters Company Officers 5 Enlisted Personnel 60 | Engineers Company Officers 7 Enlisted Personnel 100 | Airborne Regiments (3) Officers 200 ea. Enlisted Personnel 2,300 ea. | Signals Battalion Officers 40 Enlisted Personnel 250 | Chemical Warfare Company Officers 8 Enlisted Personnel 80 |

Table of Personnel and Major Equipment

Personnel/Equipment	Total Abn Div	Div Hq	Hq Co	Gd Co	AA Co	Eng Co	Recon Co	CW Co	Sig Bn	Arty Bn	Three Abn Regts (Total)
Officers	799	90	5	8	8	7	8	8	40	25	600
Enlisted Personnel	8,300	430	60	90	90	100	100	80	250	200	6,900
Total Personnel	9,099	520	65	98	98	107	108	88	290	225	7,500
7.62mm LMG	259			5		7	7				240
7.62mm HMG	75										75
14.5mm AAMG	15				3						12
60mm Mortar	45										45
82mm Mortar	45										45
120mm Mortar	9									9	
40mm AT Grenade Launcher (RPG)	516+										516+
82mm Recoilless Rifle	75										75
37mm AA Gun	5				5						
Gas Mask/Protective Clothing	189							90			99
Radio, Manpack	307									7	300
Radio, Portable/Manpack	28				8		2		18		
Radio, Vehicle Mounted	3								3		
Truck, Cargo	105	25		5							75
Truck, Utility	2								2		
Parachute, Main	8,511	110	32	98	80	90	90	70	216	225	7,500
Parachute, Reserve	8,511	110	32	98	80	90	90	70	216	225	7,500

Postscript

1987, Lewes, Sussex

In that near forgotten relic of Maoist thought, *The Little Red Book*, Mao Tse-tung said more than forty years ago: 'Without a People's Army, the People have nothing.' He gave them a People's Army, a peasant millet-and-rifle army which grew out of the Nanchang Uprising, some sixty years ago. But once the current reforms within the People's Liberation Army are complete, I doubt if Mao, the great revolutionary, would be able to recognize it. Numerically, China is already a military force to be reckoned with, certainly without equal in South-East Asia, but her re-shaped military, when complete, will have dramatic and far reaching influence; it will make China into one of the world's three great military powers, alongside the United States and the Soviet Union.

China has set her sights on being a major world power by the turn of the century and the radical transformation of the PLA, which is already in motion, is inextricably linked to this objective. Of course China's bid to become a world power depends upon the success of her current doctrines involving agriculture, industry, science and technology, and defence – the Four Modernizations. But there are two other over-riding factors which will determine China's future; internal stability, and the ability to purchase the technology the military so urgently needs.

Since coming to power Deng Xiaoping has tried clipping the wings of the PLA by refusing to stimulate the military budget. This was his way of enforcing the questionable doctrine that it is the Party that controls the 'gun' and so edge the military out of the political spotlight. There are those within the Party and the PLA who realize that this strategy has now run its course, consequently the military are beginning to dig their heels in. With the kind of military hardware that the PLA have been acquiring in recent months, it would appear that spending is once again on the increase. Deng is also preparing the ground for the PLA's modernization programme which involves retiring many of the country's old generals to make way for a new officer corps and at the same making everyone in the military better educated in order to meet the demands of advanced technology.

The People's Army as developed by Mao will be a thing of the past if Deng's policies succeed, and there is every indication that they will. Deng and his comrades have made sure that they are in control where it matters. He is Chairman of the two bodies which have the most influence in China's military direction: the Central Military Commission and the Party's own Military Commission. However, regardless of the skill with which Deng has laid his plans for the future, much will depend on who inherits from him the mantle of leadership. Whoever it is, his continued ability to manipulate the PLA will be essential if China is to achieve her planned military objectives.

Modernization of the PLA also depends on the success of China's economy. Regardless of the endless stream of tribute-bearing arms salesmen making their way to Peking, China will be cautious with her spending. To obtain the technology she needs, China is not above brain-picking what she requires from those who come bearing gifts.

She has a thriving arms business which produces some excellent weapons and military equipment through Norinco, her national arms-producing company which for some years now has been increasing its exports to a growing number of countries, including Pakistan, Tunisia and Egypt. Although China's arms sales are no more than three per cent of the world's total, combined with her other exports and investments they will enable her to supplement most of what she needs to modernize the PLA. The West must not underestimate China's ability to supply her own military requirements, through her innate ability to improvise. After all, we have to look no further than the armies of the Long March for proof of this.

After years of being the underdog in South-East Asia, China knows that she now has the potential to dominate the whole area. With the repossession of Hong Kong her strategic and economic influence throughout the Pacific will be immeasurably increased.

Britain's residency in Hong Kong does not terminate for another ten years yet Peking has already begun to pull the political strings and bring her influence to bear within the colony. Censorship is starting to threaten freedom of speech in the press and certain areas of television and film production. By invoking old legislation, the Hong Kong government wishes to minimize any criticism of Peking for fear of alienating their future rulers. Naïve indeed is the person who believes that the colony will continue its role as the capitalist jewel in Asia once the Communist take-over is complete on 30 June 1997. To put it another way: regardless of the undertakings negotiated between Whitehall and Peking on Hong Kong's future, this agreement has just as much chance of success as a unit of the People's Liberation Army hoping to be incorporated into the Brigade of Guards.

There is a further complication: the West, principally the United States, Britain and France, is supplying military equipment and technology to the People's Republic which could ultimately give China unrivalled superiority in the region – in particular, domination of the skies. Understandably, the supply of technology able to bring about a destabilization of the area is causing consternation among our friends in Japan, Taiwan and South Korea. Perhaps some form of regulation should be considered by the West when selling arms technology to China to order, to minimize any possibility of a South-East Asian confrontation.

Taiwan is a prime target for any Chinese expansionist programme and in the future can expect to come under increasing pressure to reunite with her mainland comrades and let bygones be bygones. The question then arises: in the event of the PLA invading Taiwan and taking it by force – which she is quite capable of doing – would the West then intervene?

Conversely, there are some analysts who believe that there are certain Western nations who would be prepared to deliver Taiwan into the Peking fold if their treachery would guarantee them the opportunity to play off China against the USSR. North Korea is also very adept at playing a double-facing political power game: they endeavour to play the Soviet Union off against the Chinese and the Chinese against the Soviets. However, as China's economic and military strength matures, North Korea may ultimately solicit China's support in their long-standing bid for a reunified Korea. As things are in the region, it would appear that the United States would far rather see a united Korea under Chinese influence than any Korean alliance with the Soviet Union. The ever-cautious Chinese, in their attempts to appear detached, will tend to favour the middle ground, appearing neither to favour the American nor the Soviet attitudes, sprinkling their favours a little bit in this direction and a little bit in that.

According to Bob Sloss, a leading Sinologist and Dean of Darwin College, Cambridge, what the Chinese do not wish to see developing in Asia is a rearmed Japan. He is ready to point out that one of the main purposes of the PLA is to act as a counterforce to a resurgent Japan, which he considers a potentially greater source of political tension in the area than anything which could develop between the Soviet Union, America and China. As China increasingly becomes more powerful in one part of the Pacific, the United States will withdraw to their one remaining base there – the Phillipines. Once again, he suggests, the age-old problems and tensions between Japan and China could erupt.

It is a view which I share. China's current relaxed mood is to be treated with caution. In the meantime the Chinese are attempting to broaden their sphere of influence around the world, especially in Third World countries. For China does not have to be a global power to bring about regional changes. Visitors and, in some cases, professional China watchers are all too easily seduced by the Middle Kingdom and get a fixation of what they want to see there. 'It is surprising the number of people who go to China expecting to find it a bit like "willow pattern" or the China of Marco Polo,' says Bob Sloss. What he finds totally irrational is the attitude of some visitors to China in their rather sickly adulation of the country's achievements which, although not trivial, are not in any sense remarkable. He maintains that relations between the West and China will only become healthy when people apply to the Chinese exactly the same standards that they would apply to any other people. 'While we maintain this false attitude towards China, we are going to make mistakes all the time.' He believes that we are partly to blame for it ourselves, though not entirely. 'The Chinese bait the trap for us – they want us to fall into this trap, and most of us do.'

As I see it, we in the West are concentrating all our thoughts and political manoeuvrings on a Soviet threat in Europe from either nuclear or conventional forces. Regardless of the economic and political upheavals of the past three decades, China has succeeded in producing a modest arsenal of nuclear weapons and delivery systems. Undoubtedly, China will continue to develop nuclear technology, along with their conventional weaponry, contributing further to the strategic imbalance of military influence in Asia.

Perhaps Europe and the NATO powers should be looking to South-East Asia and the future intentions of the Chinese and the People's Liberation Army? By the end of the millennium China should be in a position to exert a significant economic and military impact on global affairs.

Meanwhile, China and her people will continue to bewilder and mesmerize the West, as she has done through the centuries.

INDEX

Page numbers in italics refer to photo illustrations.

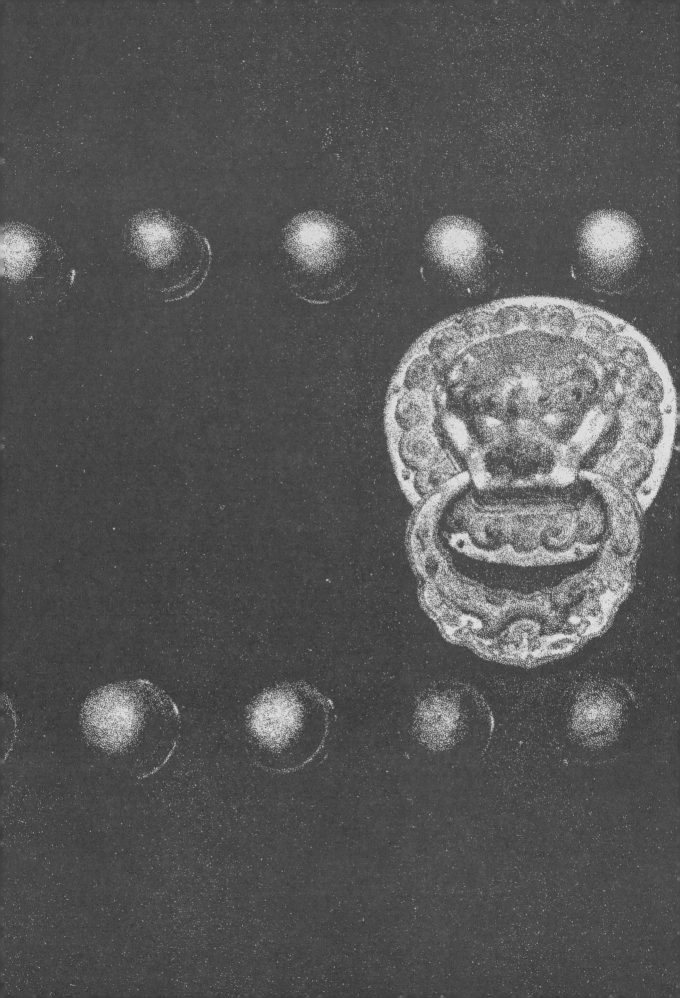